HOW TO HIRE THE RIGHT PERSON THE FIRST TIME

To Barb

Keep on making your own good fortune!

all the Best!

03/11/93

DENIS L. CAUVIER

HOW TO HIRE THE RIGHT PERSON THE FIRST TIME

Nova Personal Development Publishing
Enfield, Nova Scotia

Dedication

To my wife Debbie for her love,
energy and belief in me.

ISBN 0-88999-472-2
printed by
LANCELOT PRESS LIMITED
Hantsport, Nova Scotia
for
NOVA PERSONAL DEVELOPMENT PUBLISHING
Enfield, Nova Scotia
Canada
1990

A Personal Note From Denis Cauvier

The ability to hire the right person the first time is an invaluable asset for any manager. This book presents what I have learned about this ability, having conducted over 3,000 selection interviews and widely discussed the subject with many colleagues. This combined experience has come after years of trial and error, and many setbacks.

Use this book as a reference. A grasp of the fundamentals is sufficient to begin applying the principles of hiring. My intention is to provide a practical guide that can assist you in the selection of personnel.

Denis L. Cauvier

Foreword

I have a high regard for Denis Cauvier and the points he makes in his book, *How to Hire the Right Person the First Time*. After reading this book, I am sure you will agree that this material is both timely and practical. But more importantly, you will have at your finger tips, a relevant, hands-on guide to finding and keeping good staff.

There are a few books available on the topic of Personnel Selection, but *How to Hire the Right Person the First Time* is different. Denis takes the time to illustrate how hiring the *wrong* person will have a negative impact on your business. He also provides a wealth of practical ideas to ensure that you don't suffer from the high cost involved in making the wrong decision. Through detailed examples and ready-to-use forms, Denis gives you the tools needed to hire the *best* person the first time.

As an international speaker and the president of Newport Marketing & Communications Inc., a training corporation with offices throughout Canada, I realize the need for quick and timely information. I, and I assume you, want an author to get to the point as quickly as possible. As busy people, we look for ideas that work in the real world, not obscure theories and concepts.

In *How to Hire the Right Person the First Time,* Denis shows you step by step the process of when to hire, where to find good people, how to pre-screen applicants, as well as 56 of the best interviewing questions that I have come across.

I have had the opportunity to see Denis in action as a seminar presenter. He is an animated, knowledgeable and dynamic speaker, who takes complex issues and relates them to his audience in a simple, grass-roots manner. Denis has taken his unique style and presented it for you in this book.

Bill Gibson

Contents

Introduction

During the past six years I have been directly involved in the selection process. I have seen highly qualified and competent business people unable to make appropriate decisions in the hiring of staff. They applied tremendous amounts of time, energy, and resources towards their staffing decisions. Nevertheless, they often failed to choose the right candidates.

Hiring the wrong person is very costly. On the surface it does not seem so expensive to hire the wrong person, since he or she can easily be replaced by someone else. Yet there are many hidden costs. These costs will become apparent once we examine the steps of the hiring process, and the organizational effects of employing an inappropriate candidate.

I have developed a model which I call the hiring loop. It illustrates the various components needed to **hire the right person the first time.**

The Hiring Loop

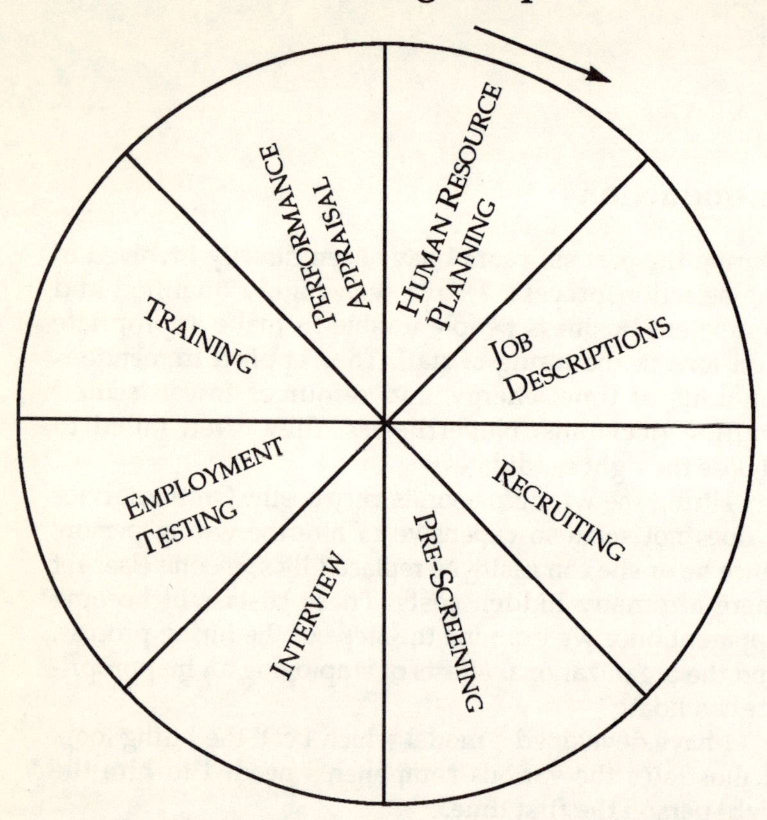

The hiring process should begin with human resource planning. By forecasting and other methods, companies can predict their future manpower requirements. It is necessary to examine the position that needs to be filled before initiating the hiring process. This process is known as job analysis. The information derived from the job analysis becomes the basis of the job description, which spells out the key duties and accountabilities of the position.

Once you know what it is you are looking for in an

employee, the next step is to attract a pool of qualified and interested applicants for the position. The recruiting process can be very time-consuming and expensive. After securing a suitable pool of qualified applicants, the selection process begins.

This process includes administering employment tests and reference checks, as well as conducting interviews to find "that right person." Even after going through all of these stages, you still have not begun to train your new employee. A tremendous amount of time is spent in training and development. The last stage is to evaluate the new employee in order to test the quality of your hiring decision. This is fostered by the performance appraisal. The cost to the company to hire the right person the first time is between $10,000 to $30,000 (according to a 1980s survey conducted by the Thomas Magnum Company of Los Angeles).

Hiring staff is a serious business. It is important to understand how these costs are incurred. The three different categories of costs can be classified as actual, potential, and hidden costs.

A. Actual Costs

• Personnel costs include salaries and other benefits for the executives, secretaries, and administrative staff involved in the hiring activity.

• Operation costs include letters, telephone calls, facsimilie transmissions, and advertising in newspapers and trade journals. It also includes travel and living expenses of both the recruiting staff and the applicant. Once the applicant is hired, operational costs include expenses for post-employment medical examinations, company literature and brochures, and testing, when applicable.

• Overhead costs include a portion of both office space, rental and the cost of furniture and equipment.

• Orientation costs refer to the administrative cost of

adding the new employee to the payroll, the salary of the new employee to cover time spent during orientation, salaries of those responsible for introducing the new hire to his or her job, and relocation costs, if applicable.

• Training costs include the salaries of training and staff development personnel, the salary of the new employee during training, and the cost of any special materials or facilities required for training.

• Assessment cost is the cost of conducting performance reviews with the new employee, which monitor whether he or she is delivering the caliber of work required by the position.

B. Potential Costs

These are costs that could be incurred if the wrong person is hired.

• By engaging a candidate who subsequently fails, the following costs accrue: record-keeping, termination, damage of materials or equipment due to undesirable job behaviour, loss of customers, and loss of goodwill.

• By rejecting a candidate who would in fact have been successful in the job, the costs are two-fold: a competitor may gain if the employee is recruited elsewhere, and selecting a new applicant to replace the rejected candidate is time-consuming and, therefore, expensive.

C. Hidden Costs

Not only are there financial costs involved in the hiring activity. The company's morale, management, efficiency, prestige, and status need to be taken into account as well. These are the hidden costs.

So what are the real costs of hiring the wrong person? The individual incorrectly hired will most likely make mistakes and/or perform below expected standards for a period of time before the problem is recognized and resolved by management. This will cost the company money on an ongoing basis due to low productivity. When a position with considerable responsibility is filled, the cost of hiring the wrong person the first time increases dramatically. For example, a sales representative making $25,000 per year who was poorly chosen could easily cost the company several times the individual's annual salary. With the cost of hiring and training so high and the cost of failure astronomical, is it any wonder that finding (recruiting) and choosing (selecting) the best possible candidates have become a critical concern in the acquisition of any company's most valuable resource, its employees?

My purpose for writing this book is to assist you in getting started or to improve your ability to hire the right person the first time. I will, to the best of my ability, show how to invest your time, energy and money wisely so that your company can reap the highest possible rewards for your efforts.

If you follow the instructions and suggestions herein, you can avoid many of the pitfalls of hiring the wrong person. You took the first step when you purchased this book. The next step is to read carefully and apply this advice, take your time and approach your selection process step-by-step. If you try to take short-cuts, you will be short-changing your hiring procedures, and increasing the odds of making costly errors.

CHAPTER ONE

Human Resource Planning and the Selection Process

A few years ago, a large fish-packaging company was in the process of building a new plant to expand their processing capacity. After careful financial planning, construction began. However, one element was missing. No one had anticipated future staffing requirements. When the issue was raised, the newly-appointed plant manager said that they would worry about that when the plant was completed.

The progressive manager recognizes the flaw in such a statement, sure to bring on premature greying of the hair! Fortunately, most managers realize that acquiring and allocating human resources is not a process that can be turned on and off like a light bulb. This process takes time, effort, and managerial commitment. Lack of attention to this matter results in higher costs and lower productivity.

James W. Walker defines human resource planning as follows: "Through human resource planning, management prepares to have the right people at the right places, at the right times to fulfill both organizational and individual objectives." The human resource planning function involves three different factors: (1) the organization's goals, (2) the demand for human resources, and (3) the supply of human resources.

Organizational Goals

The organization's stated goals imply its future human resource needs. The bottom line questions are: (a) How many people will be needed (an increase or decrease) to staff the organization in the near and distant future? and (b) What skills and abilities will they require?

Vertical integration, market development, product development, and diversification strategies, all designed to accomplish long-term organizational goals, usually require an increase in the number of employees as well as the development of new skills. Consider the situation faced by many North American banks, which were long regarded as the untouchable giants of the financial industry, when trust companies became competitive in the early 1980s. The banks were forced to adopt a more aggressive marketing posture. Not that long ago bank employees just needed to have basic teller skills in order to serve the public. Now, the banks have invested millions of dollars to create a new breed of front line personnel, called customer service representatives.

The Demand for Human Resources

An organization's future demand for qualified people has a large impact on its human resource planning. Most companies do attempt to calculate how many people will be required ever a given period of time. However, very few companies accurately guage the supply of prospective employees.

The three principle factors that influence the demand for human resources are external factors, strategic factors, and labor factors.

External factors are comprised of four elements which influence the demand for human resources. They are: changes in the economy; social, political and legal structures; technological advances; and competition. Strategic factors are influenced by changes in budgets, sales and production forecasts, new ventures, and organizational job design. Labor factors include changes in the workforce components, such as retirements, resignations, terminations, deaths, and leaves of absence.

A vast array of forecasting techniques is used to predict an organization's future demand for employees. They range from the informal chat to the use of specialized consultants who have access to specialized computer software. Even the most formal methods for forecasting employment demands are not exact. They are still approximations, albeit more sophisticated.

The Supply of Human Resources

Once the organization has completed its forecasts for future human resource demands, the next major question is, where will all these people come from to fill the prospective openings? The two key sources of sypply are internal and external. The internal supply is existing employees who can be promoted, demoted, reclassified, or transferred, in order to meet projected needs. On the other hand, not every future position can be staffed by present employees. The need often arises to hire someone from outside the organization. When attempting to forecast the external supply of labor, it is essential to note that there are several factors which can greatly influence who is available in the labor market. These are: unemployment rates, the regional economy, and community trends.

Canada Employment and Immigration Centre (CEIC) publishes both short- and long-term labor force projections. This information is available at your local CEIC office. A quarterly publication, *Ford Occupational Imbalance Listing* (also available at your local CEIC office), estimates both labor market demands and supply characteristics.

Human resource audits and replacement charts work together to help managers "map out" estimates of their internal supply of human resources. These audits summarize each employee's skills and abilities. The summary provides the planners with a "snapshot picture" of the capabilities found within the organization's workforce at any given time. Inventories of human resources must be updated periodically to maintain their usefulness. Otherwise, present employees will be overlooked for job openings within the company. Following is a sample of the skills inventory for a fictitious company called ABC Com pany.

Skills Inventory

Part I (to be completed by personnel department):

Employee's Name ______________________________

Employee number ______________________________

Job title ______________ Experience _____ years

Age ______________ Years with ABC Company ____

Other jobs held: ________ ____ ______

• with ABC Company: Title: ________ from_____ to______

Title: ________ from_____ to______

Title: ________ from_____ to______

• elsewhere: Title: ________ from_____ to______

Title: ________ from_____ to______

Part II (to be completed by employee):

Special Skills: List below any skills you possess even if they are not used in your present job.

Skills: ______________________________

____

Machines & Tools: ______________________________

____

Duties: Briefly describe your present duties: ____________________

____

____

Education: Briefly describe your education and training background:

	Years Completed	Year Graduated	Certification
High School:	________	________	________
Post Secondary:	________	________	________
Job Training:	________	________	________
Special Courses:	________	________	________

Part III (to be completed by personnel department with supervisory input):

Evaluation of Employee

Overall: ________________________________

____

Overall readiness for position: ____________________

____

To what job(s): ____________________________

Comments: ________________________________

____

Current deficiencies: ________________________

____

Employee Signature: ____________________ Date: ________

Supervisor Signature: ____________________ Date: ________

Replacement charts are like "video" representations of prospective replacements in the event of a job opening. The information for developing the chart comes from the human resource audit. Below is an example of a replacement summary for the position of City Manager.

Present Office Holder Lloyd Katz	Age 63
Probable Opening in two years	Reason Retirement
Salary Grade 99 ($58,000/yr.)	Experience 8 years
Candidate 1 John Simms	Age 58
Current Position Assistant City Manager	Experience 4 years
Current Performance Outstanding	Explanation John's performance evaluations by the City Manager are always the highest possible.
Promotability Ready now for promotion	Explanation During an extended illness of the City Manager, John assumed all duties successfully including major policy decisions and negotiations with labour unions.
Training Needs None	
Candidate 2 Mary Dean	Age 52
Current Position Utilities Manager	Experience 5 years
Current Performance Outstanding	Explanation Mary's performance has kept cost of utilities to citizens 10 to 15% below that of comparable city utilities through careful planning.

Promotability	Needs more experience	Explanation Mary's experience is limited to utilities management. Although successful, she needs more broad administrative experience in other areas. (She is ready for promotion to Assistant City Manager at this time.)

Training Needs Training in budget preparation and public relations would be desirable before promotion to City Manager.

In short, the first step in hiring the right person the first time is to undertake sufficient human resource planning, so that the organization can decide when it is necessary to hire an employee from outside, and when an employee from within the company can be promoted.

The next chapter illustrates the value of the job description and its importance in human resource planning. It goes into considerable detail in describing two critical tools — job specification and job description — which are necessary to complete the second step of the selection process.

CHAPTER TWO

Uses of Job Descriptions in the Selection Process

After designing your organization's human resource plan, let's say you realize that you need to hire two sales representatives immediately, who were not in the original plan. Would it be advisable to hire the first two sales representatives you meet? Of course not. You would need a reference point by which you could measure the suitability of applicants. The better you understand the position you are trying to fill, the better you will be able to choose the right person — the first time. Your two primary tools for selecting the right person(s) are job description and job specification. Before you can begin to prepare either of these, you first must conduct a job analysis.

A job analysis is the process of collecting and recording the specific characteristics of a position. Through this exercise, you examine the key responsibilities and the overall make-up of a particular position. This enables you to formulate the job description and job specification, the latter of which lists the key abilities and traits the position requires. Job analysis can also benefit employee training and development, as well as wage and salary determination. Its primary use, however, is to simplify, and improve the selection of human resources.

The job analysis is conducted through a variety of

information-gathering techniques. Critical information includes the duties and responsibilities of the position, and the qualifications required of the prospective job holder. Once all the information pertinent to a given position is collected, it is analyzed. The job's relationship to other positions within the company can then be mapped.

To obtain information for a job analysis,

1) observe the current employee as the job is being performed;
2) interview the employee about the job;
3) administer a questionnaire that targets job duties, and
4) require that the employee keep a daily log of tasks performed over a several week period.

These methods, in combination, will best serve as the basis for the job analysis.

Sample Job Analysis Questionnaire
ABC Company

A. Job Analysis Status
   1) Job analysis form revised on ____________________
   2) Previous revisions on ____________________
   3) Job analysis is conducted by ____________________
   4) Verified by ____________________

B. Job Identification
   1) Job Title ____________________
   2) Division ____________________
   3) Department ____________________
   4) Title of Supervisor ____________________

C. Job Summary

Briefly describe the purpose of this job, what is done, and how: ______________________________

____

____

D. Duties

1) The primary duties of this job are best classified as:
Clerical __Technical __ Professional __Managerial

2) List major duties and the proportion of time involved:

a) ______________________________ ____ %

b) ______________________________ ____ %

c) ______________________________ ____ %

3) List other duties and the proportion of time involved:

a) ______________________________ ____ %

b) ______________________________ ____ %

c) ______________________________ ____ %

4) What constitutes successful performance of these duties? ______________________________

____

____

5) How much training is needed for acceptable performance of these duties? ______________________________

____

____

E. Responsibility

1) What are the responsibilities involved in this job and how great are they?

RESPONSIBILITY	EXTENT OF RESPONSIBILITY MINOR	MAJOR
a) Equipment Operation	_____	_____
b) Use of tools	_____	_____
c) Materials usage	_____	_____
d) Protection of equipment	_____	_____
e) Protection of tools	_____	_____
f) Protection of materials	_____	_____
g) Personal safety	_____	_____
h) Safety of others	_____	_____
i) Others' work performance	_____	_____
j) Other (specify):	_____	_____

F. Personal Characteristics

1) What physical attributes are necessary to perform the job? ____

____

2) Which of the following characteristics are needed on the job and how important are they?

	unnecessary	helpful	essential
Vision	_____	_____	_____
Hearing	_____	_____	_____
Talking	_____	_____	_____
Sense of smell	_____	_____	_____
Sense of touch	_____	_____	_____
Sense of taste	_____	_____	_____
Eye-hand coordination	_____	_____	_____
Overall coordination	_____	_____	_____
Strength	_____	_____	_____
Height	_____	_____	_____
Health	_____	_____	_____

Initiative	________	_____	_____
Ingenuity	________	_____	_____
Judgment	________	_____	_____
Attention	________	_____	_____
Reading	________	_____	_____
Arithmetic	________	_____	_____
Writing	________	_____	_____
Education (level)	________	_____	_____
Other (specify)	________________________		

3) Experience for this job:
___unimportant ___important ___months required

4) Can training substitute for experience?
________ Yes How: ________________________
________ No Why: ________________________

G. Working Conditions

1) Describe the physical conditions under which this job is performed: ________________________

____

2) Are there unusual psychological demands connected with this job? Explain: ________________________

____

3) Describe any unusual conditions under which the job is performed: ________________________

____

H. Health and Safety Features

1) Describe fully any health or safety hazards associated with this job: ________________________

____

____

I. Performance Standards

1) How is the performance of this job measured?______

____

2) What identifiable factors contribute most to the successful performance of this job? ________________

____

J. Miscellaneous Comments

Are there any aspects of this job that should be especially noted? Explain: ______________________

____

____

____________________	__________________
Job Analyst's Signature	Date Completed

Once the job analysis is completed, a summary of the job's duties and responsibilties, its relationship to other jobs in your organization, and the required knowledge and skills have been identified. At this point you have all the raw data necessary to prepare the job description and the job specification.

The job description is a written account or record of a specific job. It describes its duties, tasks, and responsibilities. It also indicates how this job ties in with other jobs in the company. Keep in mind that all job descriptions within an organization must be standardized. This is not only for purposes of consistency, but also to reduce the risk of labor suits being brought against your company in the future.

Following is a sample job description:

Job Description

Identification:
Job Title: ________________________________
Division: ________________________________
Department: ________________________________
Title of Supervisor: ________________________________
Date Last Reviewed: ________________________________

Job Summary: (Briefly describe the purpose of this job, what is done and how.) ________________________________
____
____

Results: (Describe the expected results achieved from having this job performed.) ________________________________
____
____

What is the most difficult/demanding part of this job?
____
____

The experience that is required to do this job is: ________
____
____

The qualifications and/or training required for this job are: ________________________________
____
____

(Instructions: Divide the position into three key areas of responsibility. Each area of responsibility should be divided into one to five principal duties. List the knowledge and skill required for each duty. Also include the equipment and tools required for this position and the knowledge and skills required.)

I. Responsibility: ______________________

Approximate % of time: ______________________

Duties	Knowledge and Skills Required
• ______	• ______
• ______	• ______
• ______	• ______
• ______	• ______
• ______	• ______

Equipment & Tools Required	Knowledge and Skills Required
• ______	• ______
• ______	• ______
• ______	• ______
• ______	• ______
• ______	• ______

2. Responsibility: ______________________

Approximate % of time: ______________________

Duties	Knowledge and Skills Required
• ______	• ______
• ______	• ______
• ______	• ______
• ______	• ______
• ______	• ______

Equipment & Tools Required	Knowledge and Skills Required
• ______	• ______
• ______	• ______
• ______	• ______
• ______	• ______
• ______	• ______

3. Responsibility: ______

Approximate % of time: ______

Duties	Knowledge and Skills Required
• ______	• ______
• ______	• ______
• ______	• ______
• ______	• ______
• ______	• ______

Equipment & Tools Required	Knowledge and Skills Required
• ______	• ______
• ______	• ______
• ______	• ______
• ______	• ______
• ______	• ______

PREFERRED PERSONALITY PROFILE

Strengths — On the job, individuals strong in this dimension tend to be good at:

______ ______

______ ______

______________________ ______________________

______________________ ______________________

______________________ ______________________

______________________ ______________________

______________________ ______________________

Individuals who score low tend to have difficulty in the above areas.

Difficulties — On the job, individuals strong in this dimension can also tend to be:

______________________ ______________________

______________________ ______________________

______________________ ______________________

______________________ ______________________

______________________ ______________________

Cauvier/Quinlivan-Hall

A job description is normally comprised of seven different sections. The sections are broken down as follows: job identification, job summary, job duties and responsibilities, accountabilities, job dimensions, critical incidents, and job specifications. The job identification section contains the following useful information:

- Date last reviewed: The date is very important. It tells future users how old the description is. The older the description, the less likely it is to reflect the job's current status.

• Title of supervisor: The supervisor's title should be listed to help identify where the job fits into the organization as a whole.

• Location: The department where the job is located helps to identify the job for future reference. Location references may include geographic locale, divisions, plant, or other organizational breakdowns.

The job summary is a concise summary of a particular position. It tells what the job is, how it is done, and why. Within the job summary, the job duties and responsibilities describe the specific tasks of the position. Each job can be broken down into several key responsibilities. Each responsibility can be further broken down into several duties. *The job duties section is the most extensive component of the job description.* The job duties should be listed in descending order, beginning with the duty that occupies the most time.

The language used in describing job duties should be as objective and measurable as possible. Another progressive way of breaking down job duties is to organize each function into three categories of performance, such as unacceptable, minimally acceptable, and outstanding. By dividing the duties in this manner, it is easy to highlight specific examples of desired behavior for that position.

The last component of the job description is the job specification section. Job specifications are designed for the same purpose as specifications for buildings, bridges, etc. They indicate the materials needed to get the job done. Job specifications describe the education, experience, and skills the job holder requires. The last component of the job specification identifies personality characteristics and attitudes consistent with the specific position.

Once all of this information has been compiled, you have a complete job description. You have taken the time to analyze the job and to create the job description and job specification. Now you are ready to take the next step in hiring the right person the first time — recruiting qualified applicants.

CHAPTER THREE

Effective Recruiting: How to Attract Qualified Applicants

Recruitment is the process of finding and attracting applicants with certain skills, abilities, and other personal characteristics so that they will apply for employment with your organization.

A company's success in recruiting stems largely from how it makes the labor market aware of its opportunities. The effectiveness of a company's recruiting program can be measured by its ability to hire competent people. The only people available for hire are the ones attracted through recruiting efforts.

There is no one best recruiting technique; recruitment depends on the situation. Job requirements and organizational and environmental constraints all influence the recruiter's job.

Finding new employees is a continuing challenge for most companies. It is desirable for the recruiter to know personnel requirements well in advance of the new employee's start date. Proper recruitment and selection takes time. In many cases, it means the difference between getting competent, trained employees and accepting novices.

There are two major types of recruiting methods. These are: a) the search for suitable candidates from within the company, and b) the search for candidates outside the company.

Some companies have a policy whereby an initial attempt is made to fill positions from within. Besides reducing costs associated with external recruiting efforts, such "promote-from-within" policies serve to: boost employee morale; attract recruits looking for jobs with advancement opportunities (which, in turn, has the effect of helping the company to retain its present employees); and reduce training costs, since the employee is already oriented to the organization.

If the attempt to recruit internally fails, the recruitment effort then focuses on the external labor market. Generally, recruiting for lower-level positions (for example factory and office workers) is done locally, or within the boundaries of the local transit system. The search to fill higher-level positions (such as professional and managerial) often takes the recruitment effort to areas further away from the company's location. Once the recruiter has determined where to look, the best channels of recruitment must be chosen.

Recruiting methods may be grouped into two general categories: short-term and long-term techniques. Short-term techniques are designed to stimulate an immediate flow of applicants. Examples of such techniques include: newspaper advertising, spot radio advertising, and prize contests (wherein employees are awarded a cash bonus if a recruit they have referred to the company becomes a successful applicant for an existing vacancy). Long-term techniques involve public relations activities, which are designed to convince the community that the company is a desirable place in which to work. These include: plant visits, distribution of promotional literature, and the ongoing development of contacts with customers and retail outlets. By selecting one or more of these methods, a company can tailor its recruiting efforts to satisfy the company's current and future personnel requirements.

Overview of Main Sources of Short-Term Recruitment

Source	Pros	Cons
Own Staff	• Individual is known • Promote from within policy • Knowledge of the company • Economical	• Limited choice • Lack of outside experience
Former Staff (If they left for acceptable reasons)	• Individual is known • Knowledge of the company • Economical	• Limited choice • Difficulty with former colleagues
Employee Referrals	• Applicants have a realistic expectation of job and company	• Limited choice • Embarrassment if rejected • Embarrassed if hired, then later fired • Could lead to charges of creating "old boys' club"
Canada Employment Centre	• Wide coverage • Offers many related services (ie. counselling, aptitude and skills assessments, training and referrals)	• Slow to respond • Lacks resources to prescreen applicants

Private Employment Agencies (permanent placement and temporary help agencies)	• The 10% fee can cost less than if the company conducts its own search	• Limited choice • Outdated lists • Poor fit to job description and job specification
Executive Search Firms	• Access to various national and international networks	• They sometimes pursue avenues considered "unacceptable" by some companies' standards
Educational Institutions	• Minimum standards of intellect and knowledge of graduates.	• Little previous work experience
Walk-ins	• Available for work • Wants to work for your company	• May not have opening • Many will not be suitable
Newspaper Ads	• Wide choice of applicants	• Large number of applicants • Poorly designed ads will not attract quality applicants
Professional Associations	• Good for hard-to-find, highly skilled people	• Limited choice
Labour Organizations	• Use of union hiring hall to attract pretrained workers	• Not a source for "non-union shops"
Military Personnel	• Extensively pretrained, highly skilled labor	• Only have access to personnel that has previously left or is in process of leaving military

While it is essential for the company to attract a much larger number of applicants than the number of positions for which it is actually recruiting, the company must also be concerned with the quality of people who are attracted. It may be that a person who is hired turns out to be a marginal performer, but he or she was the best applicant of all those who applied. The fact that the company wound up with a marginal employee may not have been due to any shortage in the labor market, nor a defective selection decision. Rather, not enough high-caliber applicants were attracted. A recruiting program which is carefully tailored to company needs improves the caliber of applicants and ensures that more of them will possess the basics needed to perform the job.

Principles of Effective Recruitment

No single recruitment technique is effective at all times, under all circumstances, and for all companies. Most companies have found they must be prepared to quickly adapt their methods to the constantly changing character of the labor market. Before preparing the actual recruitment plan, the recruiter must be aware of any constraints arising from within the company or even from the prospective employee's immediate supervisor. The most common recruitment constraints arise as a result of company policies, whose objectives may be unrelated to recruitment per se, such as promoting uniformity, public relations considerations, and so on. Some examples of this follow.

1) The promote-from-within policy, as previously mentioned, is intended to give current employees the first opportunities for job openings. While such a policy limits the flow of new people (and their ideas) into the company, passing over employees in favor of outsiders would risk employee dissatisfaction and turnover;

2) Compensation policy dictates pay ranges for different jobs within the company. The pay range will either

motivate or discourage the recruit from becoming a serious applicant;

3) Employment status policy restricts the hiring of part-time and temporary employees. Ultimately it forces the recruiter to concentrate on full-time applicants;

4) International hiring policy, mandates that local citizens be hired to fill foreign job openings.

Through skills inventories and promotion ladders, human resource plans often summarize recruiting needs by outlining which jobs are to be filled by recruiting externally and which ones should be filled internally. The recruiter may also check the affirmative action program within the company for further guidance.

Finally, the recruiter's habits must be scrutinized regularly to guard against self-imposed constraints. Habits can develop due to past successes. Conversely they may permit past mistakes to be perpetuated.

Optimally, recruit efforts are carried out on an ongoing basis. A company which puts on a big recruiting campaign to fill a number of vacancies will continue to attract a large number of applicants even after those positions have been filled. How these late applicants are handled will affect the outcome of subsequent recruiting campaigns. Rather than turn these late applicants away, the company should process the overflow by keeping their applications in a pool for subsequent openings. As many as half of them may no longer be available when called. However, such action will build goodwill, and may provide needed people in an emergency.

It is best to avoid big recruiting campaigns entirely in favour of conducting an ongoing search effort. By doing this, companies have a ready "pool" of qualified applicants to draw upon as the need arises. Agencies, schools, and professional societies have proved helpful in recruiting for certain job categories and at particular skill levels. Maintaining contact with such recruiting sources, even during slow periods of recruitment activity, encourages them to bring outstanding candidates to the attention of the company for present and future needs. These sources may also become more willing to put in extra work or emergency assignments.

Recruitment is a marketing function, since it is really a process of selling jobs to prospective employees. While the company is out to "buy" the best possible candidate from a pool of applicants, it must be able to successfully "sell" the applicant on a belief that a desirable vacancy exists in a first-rate company. (At the same time, recruiters must avoid overselling applicants, since this can lead to employee disillusionment, resulting in labor turnover. An accusation of 'false advertising' can do extensive damage to the firm's reputation, which could adversely affect future recruitment endeavors.) Recruitment activity should, therefore, be creative, imaginative, and innovative. For example, proper word choice in recruiting materials is essential. Words such as "rapidly expanding," "nationally known," or "leading" to describe the company do more to attract potential recruits than "old" or "big." The style of recruiting material should be simple and direct, answering the applicant's primary question: "What is in it for me?" It is advisable to personalize the material through the use of such pronouns as "you" and "your."

Optimum recruiting encourages likely prospects to apply to 'your' company even before there is an opening. Chances are that a desirable employee will not be interested in buying a vaguely or improperly advertised "product" (job and company). Many well-qualified people are already employed, and they are not actively seeking new jobs, so they can not be expected to routinely investigate new opportunities. Their interest may be momentarily piqued by a recruiting message, but it will quickly fade unless the company provides some immediate and simple means of making contact. Many companies pay special attention to the timing of their recruiting messages, in order to facilitate contact. In general, the greater the competition for good employees, the easier it should be for them to apply to your company.

For most people, telephoning is easiest, followed by making an appointment. Writing a letter or summary is probably the most difficult. Specifically, when responses must be addressed to a box number (blind news ad) rather than to a known company, the applicant feels at a disadvantage because he or she does not know exactly what style of presentation is desired. Also, applicants may be more reluctant to respond to a blind ad for fear they may be applying to their present employer. This is not to say, however, that the blind ads are never suitable, particularly for top-level executive and managerial jobs. Sometimes, it is unwise for a company to identify itself before the initial contact.

If a company is undergoing a period of hiring restraint, a recruiting message that is placed openly — due to the lack of available recruits for an essential position which must be filled — would only confuse the public, since it would contradict the previous information regarding the company's hiring practices.

Advertising is a widely used source of recruitment for most managers. Some managers will, at some time in their career, become involved with this avenue of recruitment, and therefore it should be given special consideration.

The recruiter must ask a fundamental question: "What are the objectives of the advertisement?" Typically, there are five main objectives of recruitment advertising:

1) to attract suitable candidates for the job

2) to motivate appropriate readers to apply

3) to eliminate those readers who are not appropriate for the job

4) to reach appropriate candidates as economically as possible

Advertising Draft Form

Position ______________________________ Salary ____________

Location of Position ____

Paper to be run in: ____

____

____

____

Dates ad to be run: ____

____

____

____

Location to reply to: ______________________________________

____

____

____

Telephone: ____

Specific Person to Contact: _________________________________

Job Requirements: ____

____

____

Experience Required: _______________________________________

____

____

____

5) to enhance the overall reputation of the company by the image projected in the advertisement.

Following are some commonly used advertising techniques, developed to get greater pull from recruiting efforts:

1) "Off-day" and "off-season" recruiting is often overlooked by one's competitors. Running a newspaper advertisement on days when readership is down might very well attract more respondents than if the company were to compete with many similar ads during peak readership. Other examples are: visiting colleges early in the fall or even during summer sessions, to recruit engineers and other trainees; seeking out seasonal employees well in advance of the rush period; and placing late night spot radio ads.

2) A relatively recent recruiting technique called "The Sunday Special" consists of a Sunday recruiting message which invites applicants to call at once (on Sunday). This approach captures the greater readership or listenership, on their day off, and it gives the company a twenty-four-hour jump on its competitors. "The Sunday Special' catches applicants in their most receptive mood, when they have time to make a telephone call from the privacy of their home without interrupting their normal business activities.

3) Combined classified and display advertising is an effective one-two punch. The company runs a classified ad which merely refers the reader to the display ad featured in the same edition. This attracts the attention of every potential applicant.

4) A telephone call is a handy way for the applicant to make initial contact with the company, during which he or she quickly obtains a feeling for the job and whether or not it is worth pursuing. For the employer, the telephone response provides a convenient and inexpensive way to screen applicants. A structured screening questionnaire

completed during the telephone conversation allows the company to create a short list of the most promising candidates. The telephone response is especially advantageous for recruiting tours to various cities. It is much more cost-effective than having the recruiter wait in town until written responses arrive. It also reduces the risk of the best candidates no longer being available after the lag time created by the postal system.

The foregoing techniques help the recruiter get a jump on the competition, which contributes to the success of the recruitment effort. This is particularly important in tight labor markets, where one must also take into account some of the more subtle psychological aspects of recruitment. A good recruiter is always aware of what his or her competition is doing, and is alert to new ideas from all sources.

Post-Recruitment

The recruitment process ends when an applicant formally applies for employment with the company, usually by completing an application form. This does not mean, however, that the work of the recruiter is completed at this point. The recruiter must obtain feedback from interviewers and managers in charge of hiring, to ensure that current recruitment efforts are bringing in the most suitable applicants.

Conclusion

Effective recruitment is a most challenging and demanding activity. A company's success in finding and attracting desirable candidates depends on its approach to the recruiting process.

Developing a recruitment campaign involves two major activities: advertising and employee search. Recruitment practices range from word-of-mouth procedures to advertising in national newspapers. In any case, a well-planned approach, tailored to the particular needs of the company, is essential for the success of any recruitment activity.

Recruitment is costly both in human terms and in terms of time and money. A company's recruitment activities should be continually assessed so that the company knows whether it is getting full value for dollars spent, and whether, in fact, the right persons are being hired — the first time.

CHAPTER FOUR
Prescreening, Application Blanks, Resumes, and Cover Letters

You have taken the time to recruit a large pool of qualified applicants and you only have one position to fill. Are you going to interview all ninety-two secretaries? I would hope not! What you need to do is reduce the size of this group to only three to five inverviewees. The two best ways to quickly screen out applicants who don't match your requirements are a) evaluate their resumes and covering letters, and b) study their application blanks. A second effective method of pre-interview screening is to conduct selection tests. The next chapter will deal with the issue of selection testing, while this chapter will focus on the first stage of prescreening. To help keep things in order, use an applicant log to track the number of applicants. A sample applicant log is provided on the opposite page.

Pre-interview screening allows you to quickly tell if the applicant has the basic skills and knowledge needed to perform the major responsibilities and duties of the job. *(Can they do the job?)*. The interviewing stage, for the most part, is concerned with discussing the candidate's attitude. *(Is he or she the best person for this job?)*

In my opinion there are three critical elements that the candidate must possess in order to succeed within the job.

Applicant Log

Print your name, place a ✓ mark in the appropriate column or indicate purpose of visit.

Name	New	Renew	Other
1.			
2.			
3.			
4.			
5.			
6.			
7.			
8.			
9.			
10.			
11.			
12.			
13.			
14.			
15.			
16.			
17.			
18.			
19.			
20.			
21.			
22.			
23.			
24.			

The following triangle illustrates this point.

Triangle of Success:

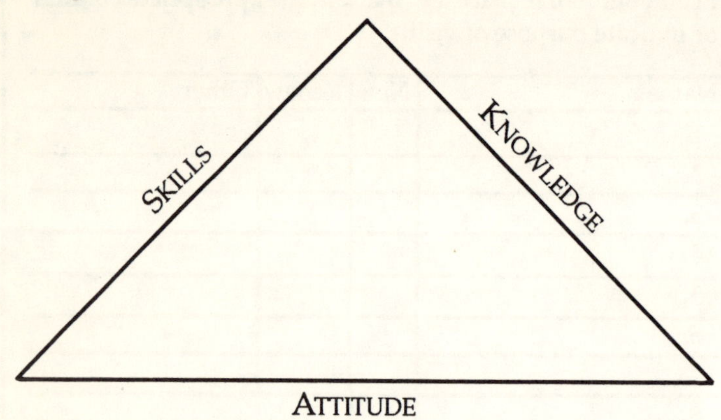

Job Skills, or experience, combined with knowledge is not enough to ensure success at a given job. The "glue" that holds everything together is attitude. For example, if I have a senior position open in sales, someone with ten years' experience (skill) and a PhD. in Marketing (knowledge) may be really lazy and disinterested in our company. That is to say, this person has a poor attitude.

Let's say I have a less senior sales position open. A young person applies who is lacking experience and does not have a degree in marketing, but he or she exhibits a great desire to be a sales representative in my company. I believe he or she will work extra hard and take home product manuals to study in the evenings, and he or she has already signed up for the weekend sales course offered at the local Chamber of Commerce. How do you think I'll feel about this young person? You're right, I would hire this person because I realize his or her potential, and also because I appreciate the fact that he or she is open to improvement.

Another way of looking at applications and resumes is

that the covering letter and resume provides you with the information that the applicant wants you to know, while the application blank provides you with the information you need to know. An effective practice in screening out applicants is to have them drop off their resume in person, if possible. Then, before they leave, the receptionist requests that they fill out the application blank, and then hands him or her a sample of the position's job description. By offering the applicant the job description and job specification, the individual will gain a more realistic view of what the job entails. He or she may no longer be interested in the job. Look at all the time, energy, and money you can save if one quarter of all your applicants screen themselves out in this manner.

Your application form should be designed to provide you with the information you need to evaluate the ability, experience, skills, knowledge, and other job qualifications of the applicant. Keep in mind that you may need to develop more than one application blank. Companies often make the error of using a blanket form for all positions. It should be obvious that the information you need in order to hire a clerk is very different from the information you need for hiring a vice-president. Your application blanks should reflect these differences. A sample of a job application blank is provided below.

Sample Job Application Blank

Job Application

(The more you write, the easier it is for us to know if you are going to fit within our company. Attach extra paper as necessary.)

1. Name: ______________________________

2. Address: ______________________________
   City: ______________ Province: ______________
   Postal Code: ______________________________
3. Telephone: (home) __________ (office) __________

Education and Training:

4. Circle the highest grade/years completed.

8 9 10 11 12 13	1 2 3 4	1 2 3 4
High School	University	Graduate School

5. Please provide the following information about your education. Include high school, trade and vocational schools, and universities.

a. School Name: ______________________________
   School Address: ______________________________
   (in Canada only)
   Degrees/Diplomas: ______________________________
   Date of Admission: ______________________________
   Date of Completion: ______________________________
b. School Name: ______________________________

School Address: ______________________
(in Canada only)

Degrees/Diplomas: ______________________

Date of Admission: ______________________

Date of Completion: ______________________

c. School Name: ______________________

School Address: ______________________
(in Canada only)

Degrees/Diplomas: ______________________

Date of Admission: ______________________

Date of Completion: ______________________

6. Special qualifications or certifications. Include name of institution, start and completion date of program, and grade achieved. ______________________

____

____

7. Industry/Business training. Include business and industry seminars and workshops.

a. Course: ______________ Date taken: ______________

Company or institution providing training: __________

____

What did you learn? ______________________

____

How did the course help you? ______________________

____

b. Course: ______________ Date taken: ______________

Company or institution providing training: ________

____

What did you learn? ________________________

____

How did the course help you? ________________

____

c. Course: ____________ Date taken: __________

Company or institution providing training: ________

____

What did you learn? ________________________

____

How did the course help you? ________________

____

d. Course: ____________ Date taken: __________

Company or institution providing training: ________

____

What did you learn? ________________________

____

How did the course help you? ________________

____

Employment History

8. a. Present employer:

Address: ________________________________

Telephone: __________ Supervisor: __________

Type of business: __________________________

Job Title: ________________________________

Job Duties: ______________________________

Why are you leaving: ______________________________

____

What would your employer say about you? __________

____

9. Past employers: Begin with the most recent.

a. Name of business: ______________________________

Address: ______________________________

Telephone: __________ Supervisor: __________

Type of business: ______________________________

Job Title: ______________________________

Job Duties: ______________________________

When did you start? (m/y) ______________________________

When did you leave? (m/y) ______________________________

Why did you leave? ______________________________

____

What would your employer say about you? __________

____

b. Name of business: ______________________________

Address: ______________________________

Telephone: __________ Supervisor: __________

Type of business: ______________________________

Job Title: ______________________________

Job Duties: ______________________________

When did you start? (m/y) ______________________________

When did you leave? (m/y) ______________________________

Why did you leave? ______________________

____

What would your employer say about you? ________

____

c. Name of business: ______________________

Address: ______________________________

Telephone: __________ Supervisor: ____________

Type of business: ______________________

Job Title: ______________________________

Job Duties: ____________________________

When did you start? (m/y) ________________

When did you leave? (m/y) ________________

Why did you leave? ______________________

____

What would your employer say about you? ________

____

Personal History

10. What are your special interests and activities? ________

____

11. What teams have you worked or played on? ________

____

12. To be an effective team player what must a person do or not do?

Do: __________________________________

Not do: ______________________________

13. What special knowledge and skills do you bring to this job? ______________________________

____

14. What are your personal strengths and weaknesses?

Strengths: ______________________________

Weaknesses: ______________________________

15. What are your personal and career goals?

Personal: ______________________________

Career: ______________________________

16. Why do you want this job? ______________________________

____

17. Is there anything else you wish to tell us about yourself? ______________________________

____

18. Can we contact you at work? ______________________________

19. If not, how do we reach you during the day? ______________________________

____

20. By my signature on this application, I:

a. authorize the verification of the above information and any other necessary inquiries that may be necessary to determine my suitability for employment;

b. affirm that the above information is true.

Applicant's signature: ______________________________

Date: ______________________________

What Should Be Included in Your Application Blank?

Your time is very valuable so it only makes sense for you to use the applicant's time, rather than your own, in the initial phases of the selection process. Encourage applicants to fill in as much information as possible on the application blanks. The more they write about themselves, the more you will learn about them. It takes a lot of time and energy to conduct one interview; in that same amount of time you can read ten to fifteen application blanks. So, make the best use of your time by allowing the applicants to screen themselves out at this early stage of the process.

Your application blank should include the following requests for information:

A. applicant's name

B. address and phone number where applicant can be reached during the day

C. position applied for

D. prior work experience

E. educational experience

F. training or skills relevant to the position

G. ability to work the hours the job requires

H. date of availability for work

I. whether the applicant is seeking full-time, part-time, temporary, or seasonal employment

J. whether the applicant has pertinent licenses or certification

K. personal history section

Personal Data

Without information on where to contact a prospective applicant, the application is not of much use. Provide space for a home phone number, a business phone number, and an address. You may also want to ask for a alternate number where a message can be left. Since it is illegal to discriminate, an unsuccessful applicant may conclude that their rejection was motivated by discrimination if discriminatory questions were asked on the application bkank, such as place of birth, marital status, number of dependents, sex, race, religion, or national origin.

Employment History

The applicant's employment history is a vital section of the application blank. You want to know the name and address of every prior employer, the job or positions held, the job duties performed, the skills required to perform these duties, the name and title of the applicant's supervisor, the rate of pay or salary, the length of employment, and the reason for leaving. This is information that you will want to review carefully and thoroughly, so make sure that you allow ample space for responses to these inquiries.

Skills and Knowledge

Include sufficient space on the application blank to gather information about job-related skills and knowledge. Depending on the position being filled, relevant responses may indicate typing ability, teaching experience, supervisory skills, or volunteer work.

Education

Depending on the position being filled, the information you seek regarding education will vary. Design your application blank to provide you with information on schools attended, dates of attendance, overall standing or grade-point average, and special achievements.

Chapter Seven, Human Rights Considerations, will address the items that should not be included on the application blank. It is recommended to have a lawyer review your application blank before putting it to use. This will ensure compliance with all legal requirements and prevent future human rights discrepancies.

Maintenance of Application Files

You have just advertised in the local paper for the position of auto mechanic. Your office had been swamped with resumes, telephone calls, and walk-ins. During a period of chaos such as this, many applications can get lost in the shuffle. You may never find a given application in your personnel files. This could lead to one of two outcomes.

1. A good candidate for the job is overlooked.
2. A candidate whose application has been lost may claim to have been a victim of discrimination, since he or she was not considered for a job for which they were qualified.

Unless you establish otherwise, all application files in your company are considered active. There is a direct correlation between the number of applications on file and the potential for confusion and future problems. There are four steps that a company can take to protect itself:

1. Only accept applications when you are filling specific positions.
2. When you are accepting applications for a particular position, state a deadline.
3. Specify the time period that a given application will remain active, and indicate this clearly for all applicants.
4. If you have separated active and inactive applications, keep them in separate files.

As I mentioned before, time is money. The most efficient use of your time is to quickly prescreen undesirable candidates prior to conducting interviews. This can be done by reviewing application blanks. There are a number of potential danger signs that one should be looking for when reviewing the application blank. I have listed seven:

1. an erratic job history with several periods of unemployemt or job hopping

2. major gaps in employment that are unaccounted for

3. salary expectations that exceed what the position pays

4. frequent changes of residence

5. a great deal of detail regarding previous experience or education which is irrevelant to the position

6. reasons for leaving previous jobs that suggest there were some problems

7. health problems or physical disabilities that would prevent the individual from performing the duties of the job

Covering Letters and Resumes

There is an old saying in advertising: Let the Buyer Beware. The same holds true for staff selection. Resumes are looking more and more alike these days, and it is becoming increasingly difficult to screen applicants. Applicants are relying more and more on the same personnel consultants and resume writing services, such that many resumes appear to be carbon copies of one another.

Remember also that resumes provide you with a one-sided look at the applicant — the positive side. Resumes, by their very nature, help applicants put their best foot forward. Keep in mind that what is *not* said in the covering letter and resume is as important as what *is* said.

Four Major Components of the Resume

The resume has four major components, each of which provides specific information that you need to consider. These areas are personal data, career objectives, education, and work experience.

Personal Data

The personal date section of the resume can offer a

tremendous amount of information. Participation in community groups or volunteer activities give insight into character and ambition. Specific hobbies and sports related to the job's responsibilities can indicate a particularly strong interest in the line of work.

Career Objectives

Most applicants include a brief statement of their career objectives in their resumes. If the applicant states the position of sales representative as his or her career objective, and the position that you are staffing is that of lab technician, the individual has probably sent out a large number of resumes to a variety of companies with the hope that he or she would "fall into a position." If the career objective statement is very vague, I would assume that the applicant has undefined career goals. An example of such a statement is "I am interested in a challenging position with potential personal growth." What you are ideally looking for is a clear, and highly focused career objective that synchronizes with the position you are currently staffing.

Educational History

The educational section of the resume contains information about the applicant's formal education as well as attendance at various seminars and workshops. One interesting point to mention is that the length and detail of the applicant's educational background is inversely proportional to the length and detail of the employment history section. Typically, university graduates with little or no experience will spend a great deal of effort to detail their educational background in an attempt to compensate for their lack of experience. The key question to ask while reviewing the educational section of a resume is: Is the educational background relevant to the position in question?

Work Experience

This section of the resume should receive the majority of your attention. It will tell you the specifics of the applicant's qualifications, experience, and career progression. Take note of unexplained gaps in employment and frequent job changes that don't indicate progression. Take heed: this is the area of the resume that is traditionally replete with cleverly disguised descriptions of job responsibilities that are in fact vague and meaningless. When reviewing resumes and covering letters, ask these questions:

1. Is the applicant profit-minded?
2. Is he or she suitable and career focused?
3. Does he or she possess ambitions?

Although a book with an attractive cover will warrant a second glance, it does not guarantee a sale. This is also true for resumes. Be on guard for "slick" resumes. Look beyond the surface appearance of the resume to the actual information it contains. For example, beware of lengthy descriptions of education that may be an attempt to hide inexperience.

Once you have gone through all of the resumes for the position you are staffing, the next step is to screen the pile of resumes. One of the quickest methods for this is to divide the pile into three smaller piles. These are the yes, maybes, and nos. Set up interviews with the yes applicants, send rejection letters to the no applicants, and place the maybes in a pending file, to be used as a backup list. An alternative method for sorting resumes is known as a selection chart.

Example of Selection Chart
(score on a scale of 1-10, 10 being the optimal score.

Applicant	EDUCATION	EXPERIENCE	KNOWLEDGE	VERBAL	SALARY	OTHER	OTHER
John Smith	6	5	1	3	6		
David Jones	2	5	4	8	4		
Mary Brown	8	7	8	6	4		
•							
•							

The selection chart identifies a number of factors pulled from the job description. List the applicants' names down the left side of the chart. Selection factors are indicated along the top. Assign each applicant a number for each factor, ranging from 1 to 10. This is a quick and effective method to determine which applicants to invite for an interview and which ones should be sent rejection letters. Once you have identified the interviewees, review their resumes and covering letters to make notes of any points requiring clarification. For example, you may want the candidate to account for gaps in employment. Unfortunately, some people lie on their resumes. Some people claim to have university degrees that they never received. Others claim to have worked for companies that never employed them. The best way to guard against such falsifications is to conduct a quality references check.

Reference Checking
It is a little-known fact that ninety percent of all hiring mistakes can be prevented through proper reference-checking procedures. Unfortunately the vast majority of employers do not take the time to do a quality reference check. Instead, these people rely on their own impressions or "gut feeling" of the candidate based on the covering letter, resume, application, and interview.This is another mistake. As I have mentioned before, hiring the wrong person can be very costly.

Checking references is absolutely essential. It is estimated that one-third of job applicants either lie on their resumes, covering letters, and application blanks, or exaggerate their accomplishments. This underscores the necessity to check references.

I have just said that the vast majority of employers do not conduct quality reference checks. Why is this so?

The number one reason, in my estimation, is that most employers do not realize how important this is. The second reason is that many employers do not know how to go about it. The third reason is that this activity can be very time-consuming. In many cases, there is great pressure to hire someone quickly.

Conducting improper reference checks has led to an increasing number of lawsuits against companies. This trend has caused employers and personnel departments to become very cautious about giving out information regarding former employees. Some companies have policies that expressly prohibit the release of employee information other than name, title, and length of employment. A question that many people ask me is: When should a reference check be conducted? It should take place prior to the interview. A lot of people conduct reference checks after the interview. In my view, this is a non-productive use of time. An effective reference check can be done in less than one-quarter of the time that it takes to conduct an interview. Therefire, if the check is done first, an undesirable applicant can be screened out, and the interview time saved.

In addition, checking references before the interview enables the interviewer to formulate questions to be asked during the interview. It is a good practice to seek permission from the applicant before checking references. A good method is to ask the applicant: Is there any employer, co-worker, supervisor, or personal reference whom you wish me to contact? Stating the question positively can yield an answer that reveals — by default — sore sports with previous employers.

Contacting the current employer is a sensitive issue. Many job applicants do not want their current employer to know that they are seeking employment elsewhere. While you do want to respect the wishes of the applicant, you also know that the current employer can provide you with a wealth of information. To get around this particular problem, let the applicant know that a written offer of employment will be contingent on receipt of a satisfactory reference from his or her current employer. (You reserve the right to withdraw the offer of employment if a satisfactory reference is not received.) By doing this, you will circumvent the problem of not being able to contact the present employer. At the same time, you will also encourage the applicant to be truthful with his or her responses, since both the prospective position and his or her present job could be put at risk by failing to tell the truth.

There are three different methods in which to check references: impersonal, by mail, and by telephone. We will take a look at each of these three methods with a focus on the telephone reference check. Although checking references in person is the most reliable and effective means of obtaining information about the applicant, it is also the least practical. Whenever possible, however, there are several advantages of face-to-face meetings with an applican-

Reference Check by Mail

_______________________________Company

To:

Attn: Employment Verifications

Please provide the information requested below and return to us in the enclosed envelope. We sincerely appreciate your cooperation.

Please fill in unshaded areas

Name		Soc. Sec. No.	Name of last Super.
The Person named indicated the following information:	**Dates of Employment From: To:**	**Last Position**	**Salary $ per**
Please indicate this information as shown in your records:	Same ❑ Different ❑ *	Same ❑ Different ❑ *	Same ❑ Different ❑ *
The Person named indicated the following information	**Reason for leaving**		
Please indicate this information as shown in your records:	Same ❑ Different ❑ *	Same ❑ Different ❑ *	

RATING	EXC	GOOD	FAIR	POOR	COMMENTS
Application of Knowledge					
Quality of Work					
Dependability					
Supervisory Ability					
Attendance					
Discipline					

Eligible for rehire? Yes ❑ No ❑ (Please explain)

Additional comments (*Please Specify)

Signature________________ **Position**________________ **Date**________

I hereby authorize The ________Company to request verification of statements made by me on my employment application.

I also give permission to the company addressed, above, to release the information requested to The Company.

____

Signature **Date**

t's former employer. In a personal meeting, you can discern the non-verbal reaction. You will also find that behind closed doors, without the telephone disturbance, people will tend to be more candid.

Checking references by mail is, in my opinion, the lest effective meant of obtaining reference information for three reasons:

1. This can be a tremendously slow process.
2. Many former employers are unlikely to fill out the form due to the time involved in writing thoughts on paper.
3. Many people hesitate to put anything in writing about past employees.

Opposite is a sample reference check by mail.

Telephone reference-checking is the most common and effective means of obtaining pertinent information about the job applicant. One advantage of this method is that it is very time effective and you can get immediate response or clarification. Although you miss the body language, since you cannot see the respondent, you can still pick up on subtle nuances in their voice. Look for signs of hesitation, tone of voice, and "long-winded" answers, particularly when you ask the critical question, "Would you rehire this person?"

Sample Reference Check

Good day, my name is   of company,   is being considered for employment in the position of   . Your name has been given as a former employer. We would greatly appreciate your evaluation of this applicant's performance. The following has been given to us. Please verify.

Employed from _____ to _____ Yes _____ No _______
Pay __________ Yes ________ No ____________________
Position held ________________ Yes _____ No _______

Please rate this applicant on the following items:

	Above Average	Average	Below Average
Performance, compared to others	________	________	________
Supervision and guidance requirements	________	________	________
Job related skills	________	________	________
Reaction to stress and change	________	________	________
Regularity of attendance	________	________	________
Meeting deadlines	________	________	________
Oral communication	________	________	________
Written communication	________	________	________
Telephone communication	________	________	________
Acceptance of direction from others	________	________	________
Acceptance of criticism from others	________	________	________
Ability to get along with others	________	________	________

Leadership qualities ________ ________ ________
Dependability ________ ________ ________
Reason for termination ______________________________
Would you rehire? Yes ______ No ______
If No, why not? ______________________________
Name ______________________________
Department ______________________________
Your position ______________________________
Relation to applicant ______________________________
Company ______________________________
Location ______________________________

A sample education verification form is provided on the following page.

If you take your time, you will find that the reference-checking stage of the selection process can save you a tremendous amount of time and energy because it will help you screen out applicants. This brings you one step closer to hiring the right person the first time.

Education Verication Form

_______________________________ Company

To:

Attn: Registrar

Date:

Please provide the information requested below and return to us in the enclosed envelope. We sincerely appreciate your cooperation.

Employee Records

I hereby authorize the school addressed above to release the information requested below.

____
EMPLOYEE SIGNATURE

Name		Birthdate	Soc. Sec. No.	Student ID No.
Dates of Attendance From To	Degree	Major (Courses taken if no degree)		GPA

Our records show the information above to be

Correct ❑ Incorrect ❑ (Please explain)

____

Signature Position Date

CHAPTER FIVE

When to Conduct Employment Testing

The employee selection process if often highly subjective and its effectiveness is hard to measure. An objective element can be added to the process to increase the odds of hiring the right person the first time: employee testing. Whether or not an organization has a testing program in place for all potential jobs, management personnel should know the advantages and disadvantages of testing.

Applicant testing has varied in popularity from firm to firm for many years. Some companies use testing as the basis of applicant screening, but most experts agree that it is not to be used as the sole criterion for candidate selection.

Testing: A Vital Component in the Selection Process

In the process of selecting employees, tests can help:

1. forecast success or failure on the job
2. eliminate subjective judgments of applicants
3. cut costs by eliminating candidates destined for fail ure
4. select those who can work effectively in your company's environment
5. identify and eliminate candidates who have a flair for doing well in job interviews.

The *type* of job will determine the usefulness of testing. Tests are best suited to jobs where:

1. Recruitment, training, and turnover costs are high.
2. the uniform skills are required, so that the number of tests does not become burdensome.
3. a clear standard of acceptable performance and unacceptable performance has been established.
4. the available applicants are plentiful enough to ensure that a good applicant can be found.
5. required skills can be identified and clearly described.
6. the required skills do not change much over time.
7. the tests are not the only measure of ability available to the interviewer.

Aptitude tests have long been used as the most accurate measure of certain ability factors. Even the most proficient interviewers can benefit from the use of tests to measure: mental ability, verbal ability, numerical ability, mechanical comprehension, clerical aptitude, and manual dexterity.

Equal Employment Opportunity regulations require a positive relationship between testing criteria and actual performance on the job. This is an intimidating factor that steers many companies away from testing.

The fact remains, however, that if no relationship exists in this respect, the test would not provide any helpful information anyway. Professionals can be engaged to help organizations validate tests. Transportability has made aptitude testing much more useful than most people realize. Transportability means that a test deemed valid for a specific job in one firm is also valid for the same job in another firm.

Two important advantages of testing are objectivity, and the means to compare applicants performing the same tasks under identical circumstances. Immediate measures of intelligence, skills, and aptitude become available, more readily than through interviews.

As with anything, the testing process has several disadvantages. Firstly, many employers put one hundred percent faith in the scores. One candidate who outscores another by a few points does not necessarily prove to be the best for the job. Even the best tests are subject to a margin of error. Clever management personnel will realize the extent of this deviation and consider its impact on the results.

Secondly, the highest score does not always indicate a match between the candidate and the available job. Many organizations repeatedly hire the highest-scoring candidate and end up with high turnover. Over-qualification can be as big a problem as under-qualification. For some jobs, management must set upper and lower limits of acceptability, in order to achieve the best match of skills and job factors.

Finally, many managers commit their biggest error by selecting the wrong test to administer. Tests which appear relevant to a specific job sometimes prove inaccurate. In order for a test to be used as a reliable measure, it must be validated by employees who currently perform the job in question.

Types of Employment Tests

A. Intelligence Testing

One of the greatest challenges in rating "intelligence" lies in establishing its meaning. One definition defines intelligence as "...the ability to use good judgment, to comprehend new concepts, to reason well, to think abstractly, to deal with language, to understand spatial relationships, and to remember well."[1] However, there are many variations.

Most professionals agree that there are five abilities

that are frequently needed on the job. These include:

1. verbal ability, or the individual's ability to use language as a tool for thinking, communicating, and planning ahead.

2. the individual's ability to deal with basic mathematical functions. Tests vary in accordance with the type of job under consideration.

3. perceptual speed. This refers to the individual's ability to recognize similarities or differences in familiar words or objects.

4. spatial ability, or the individual's capacity to visualize figures in space, as well as their relationship to one another.

5. reasoning ability, or the capacity to handle a variety of materials, words, figures, or abstractions.

Tests of mental ability provide three main practical advantages. First, since every job requires a certain level of intelligence, large pools of applicants can be screened faster and more economically than through interviews. Second, intelligence testing helps to eliminate both overqualified and under-qualified individuals, by identifying those applicants who meet the desired level. Third, people who demonstrate high scores in such tests are generally suited for high positions in the organization. The intelligence test, therefore, aids in future promotions as well.

B. Skill Testing

Each time a new employee is hired, some value should be added to the company's productivity. Knowing our applicant's skill level can help in this respect. This type of testing helps eliminate inaccurate perceptions regarding the abilities of the prospective employee.

Skill testing is most commonly administered through questionnaires and on the job performance. Criteria should be carefully developed to determine the skills needed for each position in the organization. Once this is done, skills testing can then provide two major benefits. First, candidates can be objectively ranked from "best" to "worst" in relation to the job criteria. Second, training needs can be identified and training programs can be developed with before and after tests.

C. Aptitude Testing

The ideal result of all this is for the company to use the individual's finest talents to the maximum, while the company benefits from employing the most effective employee. Many companies have developed extensive systems for measuring the talents and aptitudes of applicants.

Tests of skill are used to measure what a person has already learned about a particular job, while tests of aptitude attempt to measure the individual's capacity to learn further required skills. Scores on this type of test can often be misleading. General aptitude tests lack weighting of scores which links specific areas of the test to desired job levels. An applicant who scores highly in areas which are not relevant could easily finish ahead of a person with a lower over-all score but a higher score in the appropriate areas. A second problem arises because there is no relationship between physical abilities and the various mental abilities that are tested. Several categories of mental tests are now in general use. These tests measure factors such as: intelligence, recall, rapid learning, mechanical comprehension, comprehension of spatial relationships, accuracy or perception, and number and name matching.

D. Interest Testing

The two factors which indicate success in most jobs are aptitude and interest. Even the most qualified employees will not perform satisfactorily if they are not interested in their work. Often it takes a highly skilled interviewer to assess an applicant's interest in a certain job. However, many interviewers are not experienced enough to accomplish this. Interest tests can often reveal this far better than interviews. Interest inventories, of a sort, are established and maintained through testing. These must be updated to reflect the ever-changing interests of employees and applicants alike. Interest inventories can be used to predict what kind of job an applicant is most likely to enjoy.

The basis of interest testing lies in the fact that people who are happy and successful in a profession have common interests which set them apart from people in other professions. They can then set the standard by which the applicant's suitability is measured.

Problems arise in interest testing. Finding ways to combat these problems can be very difficult. The first problem which can arise is that applicants can tailor their responses to what they think the immediate job requires. This leads to inaccuracies in the long-term placement of employees. The purpose of the test should be explained to the applicant, and it should be pointed out that misinformation could be detrimental in the future.

By administering tests to current employees, one can develop a further benchmark for the tests. The company's top and bottom performers will be reflected in the test results, in most cases. When the tests are administered to applicants, any scores which outperform top personnel within the organization can usually be eliminated as invalid. People who try to outwit the test's purpose by supplying only the desired responses will achieve scores which are far too high to be meaningful.

E. Attitude Testing

These tests reflect the way in which a person approaches a job. Many definitions of attitude exist but they all seem to revolve around one common theme. Attitude is a function of how a person acts over a period of time, not necessarily at any given moment. Each person forms habitual ways of acting. In general, a behavioral tendency becomes a concern of a prospective employer only if:

1. it is demonstrated in an extreme way; or
2. the person seems tense or anxious due to inner conflicts.

Measuring attitude is, in most cases, a difficult task. It is generally agreed that we can estimate a person's future behavior by examining past and current behavior. The most effective way to accomplish this is by developing attitude inventories. Questions are asked that prompt a personal account of past behavior, as well as an explanation of current attitudes towards a variety of situations. Many different variations of this testing technique are in common use. These variations can be used alone or in combination to achieve the most effective results.

Temperament tests are used not only for selection, but throughout an employee's career for job redirection. Finding the jobs that will keep people happy and efficient is a very important goal for any good manager.

Test Validation

Because the validity of any given test can never be assumed, it is important to correlate tests with actual behavioral needs. Validation is the process of learning whether or not a test works. It must give the same results consistently. In other words, the test must be reliable. However, reliability alone does not ensure validity. Unreliability is often the result of how the test was constructed, or unstandardized administration. Whenever testing is done, as many factors as possible should be kept constant to ensure reliability. These factors range from the environment to the attitidue of the test administrator.

To vouchsafe reliability, there are several options. The

most obvious is to retest applicants and look for similar results the second time around. When this is done, enough time must elapse between tests so that the applicants do not remember their answers from the first go-around. Also, in avaluating the second test, we must bear in mind that some learning may have taken place as a result of the first test.

A second method for ensuring reliability calls for the use of different but equivalent forms. The level of difficulty and the general form of the tests must be the same for each test. Below is a listing of the dos and don'ts of testing.

Dos and Don'ts of Testing

Dos:

1. Warn the candidate that he or she will be tested before acceptance. If appropriate, you could give some indication of the format the test will take so that he or she can prepare for it, (eg., by reviewing his or her grade twelve chemistry notes).

2. Allow a realistic amount of time for the test.

3. Be prepared to allow for candidate stress: Few people perform as well in test situations as they would in real life.

4. Thoroughly brief the testers, trainers, and observers beforehand, so that their respective roles in the proceedings are clear.

5. Test only key elements of the job.

6. Before the testing, make sure you have a clear idea of what you are looking for, and how you are going to recognize it when you see it.

7. Make sure that all candidates have the chance to perform the test under the same conditions.

8. Brief candidates on what is required of them, what the time limits and other constraints are, and the reasons for the test.

9. Avoid distracting or interrupting the candidates during the test.

10. Make sure you apply the same standard while assessing each candidate's test performance.

Don'ts

1. Tests should not discriminate between candidates on the basis of the factors mentioned in Chapte Eight of this book.

2. Test results should not be shared with the candidate in a destructive manner. Often there is no need to divulge actual test scores. Frequently it is preferable to simply advise them that their talents would be more suitable elsewhere. Whenever possible, it is best to give positive guidance, based on test results in combination with other information acquired during the selection procedure.

A sample of an appointment for test card, to be given to the candidate, is provided below. This card serves a dual purpose. It reminds the candidate when the test will be administered, and it enables the employer to track the flow of applicants who are scheduled for testing.

Appointment for Test

Company Name: ______________________________

After reviewing your qualifications, we would like you to take our employment tests for the position of

____

Please appear in our office on ___________ , at ________ A.M., P.M. If you are unable to make this appointment, please phone ______________________________

Yours truly,

Summary

This chapter began with some background on employment testing and then provided several types of tests, together with their advantages and pitfalls. No one type of test is sufficient for most selection processes. Very few companies, on the other hand, will use all of the types of tests that have been described. Successful testing depends on proper test validation. Once a firm selects a test and validates it appropriately, the selection process should proceed effectively. By ensuring that tests remain valid we will protect the objectivity of the test instrument, which will, in turn, help us hire the right person, the first time.

Footnote:

1. Dobrish, Cecelia, Franklin, and Watts, *Hiring the Right Person for the Right Job* ((Hamilton Institute, 1984), p. 129.

CHAPTER SIX
The Interview

The principal reason for an employment interview is to determine which of the pre-screened candidates is the best person for the job. There is, however, an additional purpose: for the interviewer to tell the applicant about the job and the company.

A thought to keep foremost in your mind is that the interview is intended to narrow the number of likely prospects for a job. As an interviewer, you are going to ask yourself these key questions: "How well will the applicant fit in with the company?", and "To what degree would the company benefit if the candidate is hired?"

Five Basic Interview Formats

Interviews are commonly conducted on a one-to-one basis between the interviewer and the candidate. Group interviewers, however, are sometimes used. One form of group interview is to have the applicant meet with two or more interviewers. This allows all interviewers to evaluate the individual on the basis of the same questions and answers. Reliability is therefore improved. Another variation is to have two or more applicants interviewed together, by one or more interviewers. This saves time, especially for busy executives. It also permits the answers of different applicants to be compared immediately. The format will correspond to the position you are seeking to fill, as well as the interviewing procedures adopted by your company. There are five forms of interviews: unstructured, structured, mixed, problem-solving and stress producing.

1) The Unstructured Interview

The unstructured interview allows for the development of questions as the interview progresses. The interviewer explores topic areas as they arise in conversation. Due to the lack of control with this approach, reliability suffers, since each applicant is asked a different set of questions. This can result in a waste of the interviewer's time, and the potential to overlook areas of an applicant's skills or background.

2) The Structured Interview

In the structured interview, questions are standard and predetermined. This type of interview allows the interviewer to cover specific areas and identify the candidate's personal strengths and weaknesses. Specific answers regarding an applicant's qualifications and experience can be obtained in a structured interview. This approach improves the reliability of the interview process, but it does not allow the interviewer to follow up on interesting or unusual responses. One disadvantage of this approach is that the interview ends up seeming mechanical, and it may convey a lack of interest to candidates who are used to more flexible interviews.

3) The Mixed Interview

The mixed interview is the most widely used interviewing technique. It is a combination of the unstructured and structured interviews. In the mixed interview, the interviewer follows a predetermined plan, but deviates from it to query important details.

4) Problem-Solving Interview

Problem-solving interviews focus on a problem or series of problems that the candidate is expected to solve during the course of the interview. Both the answer and the approach taken by the applicant are evaluated. This format of interviewing is limited in scope, yet it has one advantage: It reveals the applicant's ability to solve a variety of situational problems. The actual interview might consist of ten scenarios. Following is one example. The interviewer asks:

"Suppose you notice the secretary make a copy of a computer software program, and then place the disk into her purse. What would you do?"

5) The Stress-Producing Interview

The stress-producing interview is effective when staffing positions that involve high levels of stress, such as a police officer. The purpose of this format of interviewing is to put the applicant under pressure to determine how well he or she can cope.

The technique that is used catches the applicant off guard in order to guage his or her response. This is accomplished by asking a series of harsh questions in rapid succession, and in an unfriendly manner. Since stress is usually only part of a job, in my opinion this technique should be used in conjunction with other interview formats.

The most appropriate of the following five interview formats depends on the position you are trying to staff, the philosophy of your company, and your style preference.

Structure of the Interview

The structure of the interview can best be described in five stages. Each stage has its own purpose and is intended to accomplish certain goals. An awareness of the purpose of each stage and the goals you are trying to accomplish makes the entire process smooth and effective. The five stages that each interviewer goes through are: preparation, opening, exchange of information, closing and evaluation.

Structure of Typical Employment Interview

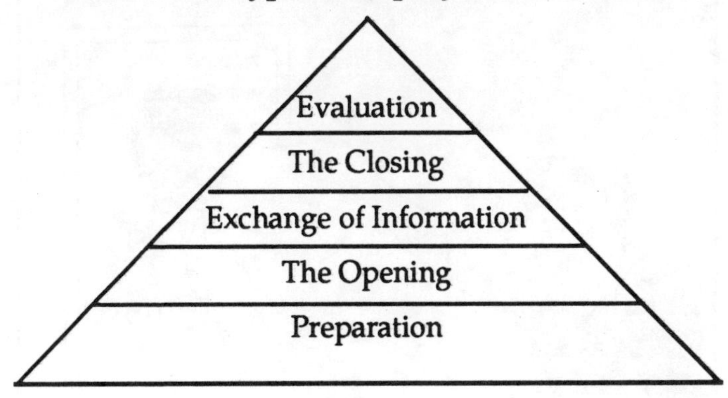

Preparation

Prior to conducting the interview, you must prepare yourself. Specific questions must be developed in advance. It is the answers to these questions that you will use in deciding the applicant's suitability. At the same time, some consideration should be given to what questions the applicant is likely to ask. Since the interview should also be used to prepare top applicants to accept subsequent job offers, you as the interviewer need to be able to explain job duties, performance standards, pay, benefits, and other areas of interest beyond the scope of the specific job opening.

The Opening

During the opening, the interviewer and interviewee get acquainted, and the interviewee is put at ease. By taking the time to help the applicant relax, you will be reducing his or her level of stress. This will help the applicant converse more freely, and you will receive answers that accu-

"Why do you want this job?"

"So, what makes you different from everyone else?"

rately reflect the true characteristics of the applicant. You can help this along by exercising typical social amenties such as: shaking hands, taking the applicant's coat, offering the applicant a chair (and coffee if appropriate), introducing yourself, and beginning with some informal discussion. The interviewer should always explain the procedure which will be followed during the interview. This serves to put the candidate further at ease by letting him or her know generally what is going to happen and about how long it will take. The candidate will also be reassured to know that there will be an opportunity to ask questions towards the end of the interview.

Exchange of Information

The body of the interview is the assessment period. Here, the interviewer fulfills the primary objective of gathering the information that will help determine whether the applicant fits the job. Obviously, the way that the exchange of information is conducted is crucial. The interviewer needs to ask appropriate questions, solicit pertinent responses, and constantly evaluate the applicant's verbal and non-verbal expressions.

The Closing

After you have solicited all the information you need to make the hiring choice, it is time to close the interview. Here, both the applicant and the interviewer have a chance to meet some of their objectives. The applicant has a chance to find out what he or she wants to know about the position, and organization, and prospective co-workers. The interviewer, in addition to answering the applicant's queries, has the chance to further evaluate the applicant's values and to attempt to sell the candidate on the company and the job, if appropriate.

Let the applicant know when you expect to make a decision and how he or she will be contacted. Being clear about the steps you intend to take will set the applicant at ease about the waiting period that will follow the interview. Be careful not to say anything that could be misconstrued as a job offer.

Evaluation

Immediately following the interview, the interviewer should record specific answers and general impressions. A post-interview report is a checklist used to record the interviewer's impressions. Using a checklist, like the one that follows, can improve the reliability of the interview or selection technique.

Post-Interview Report

Applicant ________________ Position ________________
Date ________________ 1st Interview ________________
2nd Interview ________________
3rd Interview ________________

Comment on the applicant's background and behavior, taking into consideration the elements listed in the right-hand column of each section. Then circle a rating for each section, based on the evidence you have cited. Finally, at the bottom of page 2, make one overall rating of the candidate.

<u>Initial Impression</u>
Appearance ________________________
Manner ________________________
Self-Expression ________________________
Responsiveness ________________________
Favorable 1 2 3 4 5 Unfavorable

Work Experience

Relevance of Work
Sufficiency of Work
Skill and Competence
Adaptability
Productivity
Motivation
Interpersonal Relations
Leadership
Growth & Development

Favorable 1 2 3 4 5 Unfavorable

1. Where is the candidate on his/her career cycle — going up/at the peak/going down?

2. Is the candidate's work history the result of a thought-out career pattern?

3. Has the candidate reached the level expected, given education, background and experience?

4. Have the candidate's job changes brought increased responsibilities and salary?

Education

Relevance of Schooling
Sufficiency of Schooling
Intellectual Abilities
Versatility
Breadth & Depth of Knowledge
Level of Accomplishment
Motivation, Interests
Reaction to Authority
Leadership
Teamwork

Favorable 1 2 3 4 5 Unfavorable

1. Has the candidate undertaken any course of study since leaving school?
2. Is the candidate's education sufficiently broad for the position?

Character & Attitude (Optional)

Attitudes Toward Achievement,
Work & People
Emotional & Social Adjustment
Basic Values & Goals
Self-Image

Favorable 1 2 3 4 5 Unfavorable

1. What is the candidate's attitude towards people in general?
2. Does the candidate accept responsibility?
3. Is the candidate a decision-maker?
4. Will the candidate work precisely and accurately?
5. What degree of supervision is most appropriate for the candidate?
6. Is the candidate aggressive?
7. Is the candidate flexible and willing to adapt to changes?

Maturity is an important factor of personality. A guide to a candidate's emotional maturity can be reached by considering the following questions:

1. A yes response to these will indicate emotional immaturity:

Does the candidate:

- blame others for his/her own mistakes?
- withdraw from a situation when faced with difficulty?

- make excessive claims regarding his/her own achievements?
- depend largely on the praise of others?

2. A yes response to the following questions will indicate emotional maturity:

Does the candidate:

- take his/her career seriously?
- show an ability to persevere?
- live up to commitments?
- make and stand by own decisions?
- adjust and make compromises?
- react constructively to justified criticisms?

<u>Overall Summary and Recommendations</u>

Overall rating

Favorable 1 2 3 4 5 Unfavorable

This applicant should be hired yes ___ no ___

If no, state reason: ______________________________

____

If no, would you recommend consideration at future date for this or any other position?

Yes ___ no ___ Remarks ___________________________

____

Type of work for which applicant appears best qualified:

____

Follow-up action recommended:

None ___ Additional Testing ___ Supervisory Interview ___

Follow-up interview with personnel ___

Applicant unacceptable (file) ___

Send applicant letter of rejection ___

Applicant unacceptable for job under consideration, reconsider for job as ______________________

Additional Comments: ______________________

____

____

Interview Phases

The typical interview can be divided into four equal time segments (see diagram below). The first twenty-five percent corresponds with the opening stage of the interview. It is recommended that most interviews start with a very low amount of stress. Then, slowly increase the level of stress throughout the interview. To start the interview with a low stress level you can ask some closed-ended questions. For example: "Did you have trouble finding a parking spot?" or "Would you like a cup of coffee or tea?" A closed-ended question is one that can be answered with yes or no. Closed-ended questions, for the most part, don't require a lot of thought and personal disclosure, thus, they produce low stress.

During the middle two quarters of the interview (the exchange of information phase) it is desirable to ask a lot of open-ended questions, which requires that the candidate give substantially more detailed answers. These open-ended questions are very stressful in nature. For the interviewer, this stress is positive, since it provides an opportunity to see how well the candidate performs under stress. Open-ended questions are ones that ask who, what, when, where, why, and how. These types of questions require the candidate to be descriptive.

The last phase of the interview (the closing) is used to tie up any loose ends and to reduce the candidate's level of stress. However, just prior to ending the interview it can be beneficial to once again quickly raise the candidate's level of stress through an open-ended question, like: "Why should I hire you?" The rationale for these types of questions is discussed in more detail in the next section entitled "What Are the Best Questions to Ask?"

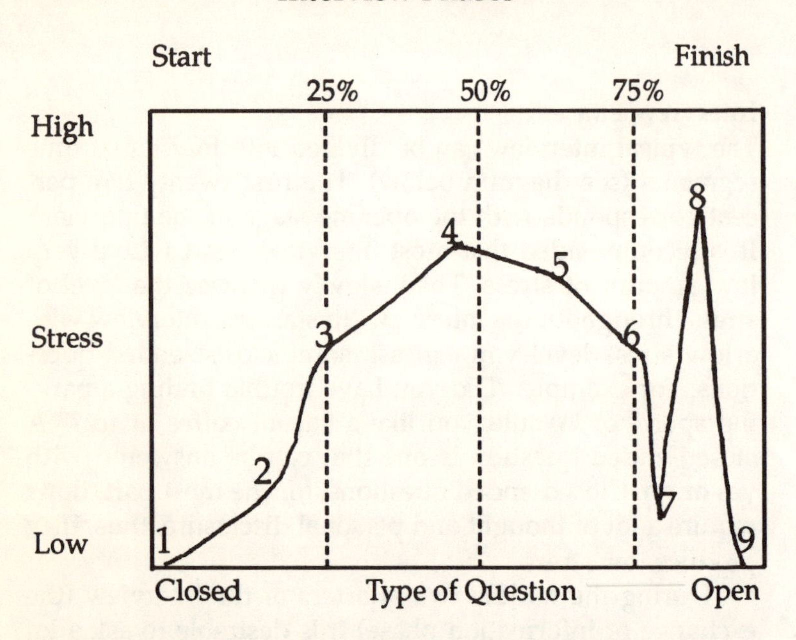

What Are the Best Questions to Ask?

Since the crux of the interview is the exchange of information, your effectiveness as a questioner is extremely important. For many people asking critical questions can be the most difficult part of the interview.

On the surface, questioning may appear to be a simple skill. However, effective questioning can take many years to master. It is unprofessional to initiate an interview without a strategy for obtaining the information you need. The position you are trying to fill will determine the kind of information you will want to collect. By reviewing the job description, you can familiarize yourself with the qualifications the position requires. It is advisable to follow a pre-planned progression of questioning. This will reduce the probability of confusing the applicant with random questions. Most typically, the progression goes from work history, to educational background, to personal and professional goals. You may decide to restructure the progression of your questions. Variations are acceptable, so long as they allow the interview to proceed smoothly.

Open-Ended Questions

An open-ended question is one that allows for an expanded range of responses. It allows you to glimpse how the applicant thinks, guage the applicant's communication skills, and scrutinize the applicant's ability to organize his or her responses.

By encouraging the candidate to answer in his or her own way, you place the responsibility for carrying the conversation on the applicant. The 70/30 rate of communications applies during the interviewing process. The interviewer should be speaking no more than thirty percent of the time. By listening and observing the rest of the time, one can learn new things about the candidate.

Questions that begin with the words who, what, where, when, why and how solicit open responses. Open-ended questions might also start with a phrase such as "Tell me ..." One of the tests of an open-ended question is that it is impossible to answer it with "Yes" or "No." Also, it does not suggest to the applicant what specific kinds of information the interviewer wants. It does not suggest what the interviewer considers is important, nor does it imply that a given answer will be considered "correct" by the interviewer. When using this questioning technique, you may be asked by the candidate, "What exactly would you like to know?" Your response should be: "I don't have anything specific in mind. Feel free to say whatever you like." When asking open-ended questions, be prepared for some silence on the part of the applicant. A few-second pause is normal. This allows the candidate to collect his or her thoughts to form an answer. You may need to rephrase questions or probe for more detail if you do not find out what you are after.

I have listed fifty-three sample open-ended questions that could be asked during the interview.

Work Experience

Cover: earliest jobs, part-time, temporary, and full-time positions

Ask:

1. Could you describe your career with ___________?

2. Tell me about your work experience in general terms, beginning with your job as ___________ and leading up to your present job.

3. Tell me about some of your achievements that have been recognized by your superiors.

4. Will you describe your present duties and responsibilities?

5. Would you tell me more specifically about your duties as ___________ with ___________ ?

6. What do you feel were some of your most important accomplishments in your job as ___________ ?

7. What are some of your reasons for considering other employment at this time?

8. How would you describe your present/past supervisor? What do you think were his/her major strengths and weaknesses?

9. What are some things your supervisors have complimented you on? What have they criticized?

10. How do you think your present/past supervisor would describe you?

11. What are some things you particularly like about your job as ____________?

12. What did you least enjoy?

13. What are some things that frustrate you most in your present job?

14. What are some of the setbacks and disappointments you experienced?

15. What were some problems you encountered on your job as __________ and how did you solve them?

16. What is your impression of (*former company*)?

17. Why did you leave ______________ ?

Things to look for:

- relevance of work
- sufficiency of work
- skill and competence
- adaptability
- productivity
- motivation
- interpersonal relations
- leadership
- growth and development

Education:

Cover: elementary school, junior and senior high schools, college and university, specialized training, and recent courses

Ask:

18. I see you went to (*school/university*). Could you tell me about your education there?

19. How would you describe your academic accomplishments?

20. Why did you choose (*subject*) as an area of study?

21. How did you decide to become a (*job title*)?
22. What subjects did you enjoy most? Why?
23. What subjects did you enjoy least? Why?
24. What were your best subjects at school/university? Why?
25. What subjects did you not do quite so well in? Why?
26. Tell me about any additional training or education you've had since you graduated from school/university.
27. How do you think high school/college contributed to your overall development?

Things to look for:

- relevance of schooling
- sufficiency of schooling
- intellectual abilities
- versatility
- breadth and depth of knowledge
- level of accomplishment
- motivation, interest
- reaction to authority
- leadership
- teamwork

Job Knowledge
Cover: candidate's knowledge and job expectations

Ask:

28. I know you don't (or do) have a great deal of information about it, but what is your perception of the job of (*job appliied for*)?
29. I see you've worked as a __________. Would you describe some of your experiences?
30. What problems did you encounter in your position as __________?
31. What qualities do you think it would take to become a successful (*job applied for*)?

32. What would you say are some of the problems a supervisor has to face?

Things to look for: accuracy of knowledge and realistic job expectations.

Personal Factors and Outside Activities

Cover:

- special interests and hobbies
- civic and community affairs
- living arrangements
- marriage and family
- finances
- health and energy
- geographical preferences

33. In general, how would you describe yourself?

34. Describe the sort of career path you would like to follow.

35. Tell me about your career goals and what kind of things you are looking for in a job.

36. What are some things in a job that are important to you?

37. What would you say there is about this job you're applying for that is particularly appealing to you?

38. What are some things that might not be so desirable?

39. Earlier we were talking about your accomplishments as a ______________. What would you say accounted for that success?

40. How about the other side of the coin? What sort of personal qualities and abilities would you like to see improved in yourself?

41. What traits or qualities do you most admire in a supervisor?

42. What disappointments, setbacks, or failures have you had in life?

43. What kind of situations make you feel tense and nervous?

44. What are your salary expectations coming into this job?

45. Can you describe a difficult obstacle you've had to overcome? How did you handle it?

46. What do you consider to be your greatest achievement? Why?

47. How do you feel about travelling and/or working overtime?

48. How do you feel about the right to strike of workers in essential services?

49. Tell me about your recreational or leisure time and interests.

50. You seem to be involved in a number of outside activities. Could you tell me about them?

51. I notice you're involved in __________. Would you tell me about that?

52. Besides __________, what do you like to do with your leisure time?

53. What do you like to avoid getting involved in during your spare time?

54. How do you like to spend your vacations?

55. If you had more time, are there any activities you'd like to participate in? Why?

<u>Things to look for:</u>

- vitality
- management of time, energy, and money
- maturity and judgment
- intellectual growth
- cultural breadth
- diversity of interests
- social interests
- social skills
- leadership

- basic values and goals
- situational factors

After asking a sufficient number of open-ended questions, it is time to close the interview. An example of closing remarks follows. "You have given me a good review of your background and experience. I have enjoyed talking with you, and I appreciate what you have shared with me. It will help us make our decision. Before we close, what else would you like to cover? What would you like to ask me about the job, or organization, or anything else?"

Once you have taken care of the candidate's concerns, you can end the interview. At this point in time the applicant starts to relax because the interview is drawing to a close. Just before the candidate leaves my office, I will ask one final question, as mentioned earlier. I ask this question because I am very interested in how the candidate will react, and how quickly he or she can summarize his or her strengths.

Overcoming Interviewer Errors

In any employment interview, there is a possibility for error. Three typical interviewer errors are: 1) barriers to effective communication; 2) asking sensitive questions during an unappropriate time, and; 3) rating errors. The following section will explore these errors and offer insights as to how they might be overcome.

<u>1) Barriers to Effective Communication</u>

Stress: The interviewer may be under a certain amount of stress because of the urgency to identify the right applicant, and then make a good impression on him or her. Usually, though, the applicant feels significantly more stress. His or her career and financial security are often at stake.

Defensiveness: If an applicant feels criticized or attacked by the interviewer, he or she will counter by resisting this attack. Not only will the applicant resist offering the specific information which would prove the interviewer correct, but he or she may feel compelled to go a step further by stretching the truth in order to disprove the interviewer. Many applicants, once they become defensive, continue in a pattern of resistance that impedes in-depth communication.

Poor Listening: Often, communication is hampered because we hear what we expect to hear, rather than what is actually being said. We listen only for what fits our purposes, or until we have "classified" the speaker's remarks in our mind. Probably, ineffective listening habits have destroyed the flow of communication in interviews more often than any other single error.

Language Difficulties: The words which are chosen by one communicator must have the same approximate meaning to the other, or communication will be faulty. In many interviews, communication lines have been tenuous because the interviewer's vocabulary was over the head of the candidate or because words with emotional connotations were interpreted differently by sender and receiver.

Sensitive Questions: In verbal communication, timing is very important. Questions or comments that the applicant may take in stride at one point in the interview may be entirely inappropriate at another point. Especially in the early stages of the interview, emotional barriers can be created by questions on a subject that is sensitive to the applicant. If the interviewer attempts an in-edpth exploration of a sensitive subject before the applicant is ready to open up, stress and resistance can set in, and the flow of communication may be adversely affected for the remainder of the interview. For this reason, start the interview with subjects of interest to the candidate. Later on, after the candidate has become more comfortable, it is often possible to probe the more sensitive areas with a minimum of resistance on the candidate's part.

Most questions that are too direct or too sensitive can be opened up if they are worded differently. Ask the question you want to ask, but not in a way that is too personal, challenging, or threatening.

The following chart contains a few examples of sensitive questions that should be asked in some interviews. This illustrates ways in which questions can be worded, in order to steer clear of emotional barriers.

Sensitive Questions and Their Alternatives

Too direct or sensitive	Less direct or sensitive
Why were you fired from your last job? or Why are you looking for another job?	What are some of your reasons for considering other employment at this time?
Did you have trouble with your boss?	How would you describe your boss?
Why did you leave school?	Was there any particular reason that you decided to leave school when you did?
To what do you attribute your poor employment record?	I see you have changed jobs several times. What were some of your reasons for this?
Did you get along with your co-workers?	Could you describe your relationship with a co-worker with whom you worked particularly well?

What didn't you like about your last job?	Most jobe have unpleasant characteristics. What were some of the unpleasant aspects of your last job?
Are you free to move?	How would you feel about moving to another city?

Rating Errors

The interview's effectiveness can be greatly undermined by rating errors. The five most common rating errors are: central tendency, halo effect, leading questions, personal biases, and interviewer domination.

Central Tendency

The central tendency error refers to the interviewer's inclination to appraise the candidate at a central point on a scale — usually the average or midpoint. This is both the most common and most serious type of error. It can result from the fear of rating too high or too low; it seems safer to cluster all scores towards the center. Thus, the interviewer avoids making the "wrong" determination about a candidate, and also protects himself or herself from appearing biased.

Halo Effect

The halo effect error occurs when the interviewer's evaluation is based on limited information. Consider: An applicant with a pleasant smile and a firm handshake is sized up as a leading candidate before the interview begins, or an interviewer mentally rejects an applicant who walks in wearing blue jeans.

Leading Questions

Interviewers who send out subtle messages which alert the candidate to the desired answer by the way the question is phrased are committing another type of error. For example: "Do you think customers are important?" and "Do you think you will like this kind of work?"

Personal Biases
Interviewers who harbor prejudice against specific groups are influenced by personal bias. This is in direct violation of human rights legislation. An interviewer who believes that some jobs are only for men, and others are only for women, is quilty of this error.

Interviewer Domination
Interviewers who use the interview to oversell the applicant, brag about their own successes or the importance of their own job, or carry on a social conversation instead of an interview, are guilty of interviewer domination errors.

As a final note to this chapter on interviewing, decisions should be suspended until all the interviews are completed. Many interviewers make the mistake of automatically weeding out applicants immediately after the interview is over — sometimes even sooner. Resist the impulse to do this and keep an open mind. Do not make a decision until you have interviewed all applicants.

In Chapter Seven, human rights considerations are explained in some detail. It is important to know the legal ramifications of the hiring process.

CHAPTER SEVEN
Human Rights Considerations

All jurisdictions in Canada have enacted legislation designed to ensure the equality of all Canadians. Human rights legislation as a whole is a group of federal and provincial acts whose common objective is to provide equal employment opportunities. These acts outlaw discrimination based on race, color, religion, national origin, sex, or age. Under special circumstances, they also outlaw discrimination against handicapped persons. However, discrimination between workers on the basis of their effort, performance, or other work-related criteria remains both permissible and advisable.

I have included in this chapter some guidelines, so that your staff selections will conform to human rights legislation. I will address nineteen different subject areas. For each subject I will identify both the unacceptable and acceptable practices.

1. Subject: Name

Unacceptable Practices
- Asking for maiden name of applicant
- Asking for previous name when name was changed by court order or otherwise

Acceptable Practices
- Asking for name under

	which applicant has been educated or employed
2. Subject: Address	
Unacceptable Practices	• Asking for foreign address (which may indicate national origin)
Acceptable Practices	• Asking for place and duration of current and previous addresses in Canada
3. Subject: Age	
Unacceptable Practices	• Asking for birth certificate, baptismal record, or any other documents or information regarding age of applicant
Acceptable Practices	• Asking whether applicant has attained minimum age, or has exceeded maximum age
Comment	• Verification of age may be obtained after hiring.
4. Subject: Sex	
Unacceptable Practices	• Asking about sex of applicant on the application form • Using different or coded application forms for males and females
Comment	• Correspondence to applicants may be addressed to their homes with or without the prefixes Mr., Mrs., Ms., eg., "Dear Mary Smith."

5. Subject: Marital Status

Unacceptable Practices	• Asking whether applicant is single, married, remarried, engaged, divorced, separated, widowed, or living common law. • Asking about applicant's spouse, e.g., "Is spouse subject to transfer?" • Asking for number of children or other dependents • Asking about child-care arrangements • Asking whether applicant is pregnant, on birth control, or has future child bearing plans
Acceptable Practices	• Asking if applicant is willing to travel or be transferred to other areas of the province or country, if this requirement is job-related.
Comment	• Information, if required for tax or insurance purposes, may be requested after hiring.

6. Subject: National or Ethnic Origin

Unacceptable Practices	• Asking about birthplace • Asking about nationality of parents, grandparents, relatives, or spouse • Asking about ethnic or national origin, eg. requiring birth certificate or asking for mother tongue

	• Asking whether applicant is native born or naturalized
	• Asking for date citizenship was received
	• Asking for proof of citizenship
Acceptable Practices	• Asking if the applicant is legally entitled to work in Canada
Comment	• An employer may ask for documentary proof of eligibility to work in Canada after hiring

7. Subject: Medical Information

Comment	• A medical examination will necessarily reveal prohibited information about an applicant, such as his or her age, race, or sex. For this reason employers should conduct medical examinations after the hiring decision is made. Employers may indicate on the application form that the job offer is conditional on the applicant's passing a medical examination

8. Subject: Organizations

Unacceptable Practices	• Asking applicant to list all clubs or organizations he or she belongs to
Acceptable Practices	• Asking for such a list with the provision that the appli-

	cant may decline to list clubs or organizations if they indicate prohibited grounds for descrimination
Comment	• The request should only be made if membership in organizations is necessary to determine job qualifications.

9. Subject: Height and Weight

Comment	• Height and weight requirements may be discriminatory if they screen out disproportionate numbers of minority group individuals or women, and cannot be shown to be essential for the performance of the job.

10. Subject: Relatives

Unacceptable Practices	• Asking for relationship to applicant of next of kin to be notified in case of emergency
Acceptable Practices	• Asking for name and address of person to be notified in case of emergency

11. Subject: References

Unacceptable Practices	• Asking any question of a person given a reference that would not be allowable if asked directly of the applicant

12. Subject: Criminal Conviction

Unacceptable Practices	• Asking whether applicant

	has ever been convicted of an offence
Acceptable Practices	• Asking whether applicant has been convicted of an offence for which no pardon has been granted
Comment	The Canadian Human Rights Act permits discrimination based on a criminal conviction for which a pardon has not been granted. However, it discourages inquiries into unpardoned criminal convictions unless the particular conviction is relevant to job qualification. A theft and fraud conviction is relevant to a job requiring honesty, but a conviction for marijuana possession is not.

13. Subject: Optional Inquiries

Unacceptable Practices	• Making any of the above prohibited inquiries, even if marked "optional" on the application form

14. Subject: Military

Unacceptable Practices	• Asking about military service
Acceptable Practices	• Asking about Canadian military service
Comment	• Asking about all military service is permissible if

military experience directly relates to the job applied for.

15. Subject: Languages

Unacceptable Practices
- Asking about mother tongue or where language skills were obtained

Acceptable Practices
- Asking which languages applicant speaks, reads, or writes, if job related

Comment
- Testing or scoring an applicant in English or French language proficiency is not approved unless English or French language skill is a requirement for the work to be performed.

16. Subject: Race or Color

Unacceptable Practices
- Asking anything which would indicate race, color, or complexion, including color of eyes, hair or skin

17. Subject: Photographs

Unacceptable Practices
- Asking for photograph, or taking a photograph

Comment
- Photos may be required after hiring for identification purposes.

18. Subject: Religion

Unacceptable Practices
- Asking about religious affiliation
- Asking about willingness

or availability to work on a specific religious holiday
• Asking about church attended, religious holidays, customs observed, or religious dress
• Asking for reference or recommendation from pastor, priest, minister, rabbi, or other religious leader

Acceptable Practices
• Asking about willingness to work a specified work schedule

Comment
• It is the duty of the employer to accommodate the religious observances of the applicant, if it is reasonably possible to do so. After hiring, inquiry about religion is permitted in order to determine when leave of absence might be required for religious observances.

<u>19. Subject: Physical Handicap</u>

Unacceptable Practices
• Asking about all physical handicaps, limitations, or health problems which would tend to elicit handicaps or conditions not necessarily related to job performance

Acceptable Practices
• Asking whether applicant has any physical handicaps or health problems affecting the job applied for

	• Inquiry as to any physical handicaps or limitations that the applicant wishes to be taken into consideration when determining job placement
Comment	• A physical handicap is relevant to the job if: (a) the handicap would be hazardous to the applicant, co-workers, clients, or the public; or (b) the handicap would prevent the applicant from performing the duties of the job satisfactorily.

What Does All This Mean To You, The Employer?
You cannot discriminate against people who are capable of doing the job, on the basis of what they look like or characteristic differences that are unrelated to job performance.

It is important to remember that legislation is not intended to keep you from hiring the person who is best able to do the job. Rather, its intent is for you to consider candidates you might ordinarily assume are unable to perform, simply because "no one like that ever did it before."

From a practical point of view, if the best "man" for the job is an Indian woman in a wheelchair, it would be poor business practice to not offer it to her.

Application Blanks
You cannot ask questions on your application blanks, nor may you make notes which might be used to discriminate. Essentially, you are restricted to asking about work ability rather than social life. Unless you can show that the applicant's social life affects the job, it is irrelevant to the hiring process.

Types of Discrimination

Discrimination in employment is divided into three categories:

a) Intentional

The employer purposefully seeks to bar certain groups. For example, an advertisement reads: "No blacks or women need apply."

b) Unintentional

The employer excludes certain groups through testing or screening procedures which have "no relationship to performance." For example, "policemen must be at least 5'8" tall." This will eliminate most women and Orientals, although it is not specifically designed to do so.

c) Systemic

People tend to hire people like themselves. When the management of an organization is composed of all white males, they tend to hire white males. "They fit in better." Recruiting is always done from the same schools which happen to be in white middle-class areas which attract that group.

The intentions here may be innocent. The company is merely trying to get people who will succeed within the organization, so they use systems which have always worked in the past. The effect, however, may be discriminatory in its results.

How Can I Avoid Discrimination?

Legislation does not make employers less prejudiced. It makes them more aware of a problem that exists. You owe it to your company to get the best people. When you interview people, try to look past their physical attributes to determine whether they can do the job. Hire the person who can best do the job; other considerations are secondary.

If you feel that a certain minority or protected group might need training in order to do the job, ask your Canada Employment counselor about grants to cover training costs. They are often available.

The human rights professionals can also help you solve a problem you may have about hiring certain groups. They want to help make it easy for you to hire these people. Their job is not to throw you in jail, but to help difficult-to-employ people get jobs. When approached positively, they can be an asset.

While interviewing applicants for a position, ask yourself this critical question: "Is this question relevant in order to judge the candidate's suitability for this position?" If the answer to this question is no, don't ask it. Besides wasting interview time, it may very well violate current human rights legislation.

Maintenance of Records

Even if you can honestly say that your employment methods are fair and you have never had any problems with grievances, you must still maintain records of your staffing practices. This is necessary to protect yourself in the event of a future grievance.

Included is a sample offer of employment letter. The benefit of sending this letter is that it stipulates the conditions of the offer of employment. The company thereby protects itself from accusations of breach of human rights legislation.

It is a good policy to send letters of rejection to all applicants who were not hired. It is a common courtesy, and a good public relations practice. Included is a sample of a letter of rejection.

This rejection letter is a form letter. It is more personal to design your own letter using company letterhead. The

Offer of Employment Letter

Company Name ________________________________

Dear Mr. ❑
Ms. ❑ ________________________________

❑ confirm our
It is a pleasure to ❑ extend you an offer of employment as

____

with ____at a starting salary of $ ______ per month. You will be working for ________________ in the ______________
Supervisor's Name Group/Dept. Name

(in/at) ________________________________
Optional/Location

Check One Only

a. ❑ We understand you have accepted this offer and will start on
____

b. ❑ We understand you have accepted this offer and will advise us of your start date by ________________

c. ❑ We understand you have accepted this offer. Please call me collect at ____________ to let me know when you plan to start.

d. ❑ We are very anxious to receive a positive answer from you and would appreciate learning of your decision. ____________

(Check one) ❑ By (Date) ________________
You may call me collect at ____________
❑ Within two weeks
❑ ASAP

Report to ❑ Your first day
❑ __________
Month/Day

________________ we sincerely look forward to having you join us.

Sincerely ________________
Name

Enclosures ❑ Yes ________________
❑ No Title

cc: ________________

important point is to humanize the hiring process as much as possible.

________________, 19____

Dear ______________________________

We are sorry to report that another applicant has been selected for the position of

____

We are retaining your application on file for future consideration, in event another vacancy should occur.

____
Signature

Once you have made the hiring decision, the next step is to orient and train your new employee. Orientation and training are essential to integrate this new employee into your organization.

Chapter Eight
Orientation and Training

Now that you have hired the right person the first time, you must help him or her begin to work efficiently as soon as possible. Although orientation and training cost time and money, to most organizations, these costs are sound investments. Newly hired employees are seldom capable of fully performing their job duties. Even individuals with experience need to learn about the organization — its people, its policies, and its procedures. They may need training in order to perform successfully. The gap between the new employee's abilities and the job's demands can be substantial. Orientation and training supplement the new worker's abilities.

Effective Orientation

There are several things that can be done to make the orientation seminar successful for both the employer and employee. The following guidelines may prove helpful.

1) Putting the New Employee At Ease

Initially you should welcome the employee and reestablish the rapport that was built during the selection process. Once the new employee begins to relax, introduce the staff to their newest team member.

2) Organization Chart

It is important for the new employee to understand how he or she fits into the "big picture," and how the chain of command operates in your company. This can be accomplished by showing him or her a copy of the organizational chart, and explaining how the departments and divisions are organized. Finally you can show the new employee how his or her department relates to the others in the company.

3) Company and Department Objectives and Personal Goals

In order for the new employee to "fit in" and be fully productive, he or she must understand the company's long-term mission, the department's objectives, and the particular goals of his or her new position.

4) Company Personnel Policies

The employee's initial questions are often about hours of work and vacation time. These issues should be covered in the personnel policy section of the company's employee handbook. I have included here a sample personnel policy from a non-profit day care organization.

Personnel Policy

1. Employment of Staff

The personnel committee in conjunction with the program director is responsible for hiring staff. Staff members are required to be eighteen years of age or over, have completed Grade XI or equivalent, and must be in good health.

2. Salaries

All salaries will be reviewed by the Personnel Committee and Finance Committee and recommendations will be brought to the Board for consideration. The salaries paid are based upon qualification and experience. All staff will be paid on the basis of twenty-six pay periods. Increments will be considered after a three-month probationary period and on the employee's anniversary date. Mileage will be paid to staff, records maintained, and appropriate claims submitted to the Director.

3. Hours of Work

The normal hours of work will be forty hours weekly, Monday to Friday inclusive. A lunch period of one hour will be granted. Two rest periods, one morning and one afternoon, each of fifteen minutes duration, shall be part of the working day. Overtime: There is no financial compensation for overtime hours worked — you will receive time off in lieu. You must take the time accumulated soon after it is incurred.

4. Statutory Holidays

All permanent employees shall be granted the following eleven holidays annually with remuneration:

New Year's Day
Good Friday
Easter Monday
Victoria Day
Canada Day
Thanksgiving Day
Remembrance Day
Christmas Day
Civic Holiday
Boxing Day
Labor Day

If a holiday falls on Saturday or Sunday, a day in lieu of the holiday will be given each full-time employee. This must be taken within thirty working days and is to be arranged with the Administrator.

5. Vacation

All full-time employees with six month's service shall receive a one week (five working days) vacation with pay annually; twelve month's service shall receive two weeks' (ten working days) vacation annually with pay; three years' service shall receive three weeks' (fifteen working days) vacation with pay annually; five years' service shall receive four weeks' maximum vacation with pay annually with stipulation that these four weeks will not be taken consecutively. All vacation must be taken within the calendar year January 1 to December 31. Vacation for part-time workers will be calculated accordingly.

6. Sick Leave

Employees may accumulate up to one and one-half sick days per month to a maximum of fifteen days per year with a carry-over of no more than fifteen days in any given year. If absent from her duties for five consecutive days, a medical certificate must be obtained. When a staff member is ill, she must advise, by telephone, the Director or an employee designated by the Director one hour prior to the beginning of her regular work day and report again every day thereafter for the duration of the illness.

7. Leave of Absence

Leaves of absence will be considered for those wishing to continue their studies in day care. Leaves of absence for other special circumstances such as death in the family, serious illness, pregnancy, conferences, shall be considered at the discretion of the Personnel Committee and the Board of Directors. This leave of absence shall be without pay, nor shall vacation and/or sick leave be accumulated during this leave.

8. Compassionate Leave

When death occurs to a member of the immediate family of an employee, such employee shall be granted compassionate leave with pay, for a period not to exceed five days. The members of the immediate family are the employee's spouse, mother, father, brothers, sisters, sons, and daughters. Extended family shall be granted one compassionate day of leave. This leave may be extended at the discretion of the Director in consultation with the Board Chairman and/or Personnel Chairman.

9. Time Off For Appointments

Time off for appointments will be granted at the discretion of the Director.

10. Termination of Employment

An employee shall forward a letter to the Personnel Committee or Director not less than ten working days prior to the effective date of termination.

11. Dismissal of Staff

The Administration, in conjunction with the Personnel Committee, may suspend any staff member immediately for insubordination, immorality, or irresponsibility. The employee has the right to appeal, within five days, first to the Personnel Committee; and if not satisfied, to the Board. Such persons need only to write or telephone the Personnel Committee Chairman to request a meeting. The Personnel Committee, in conjunction with the Board of Directors has the responsibility of disciplining and dismissal of all staff. The responsibility of staff training and disciplining may be delegated to the Administrator.

12. Staff Evaluation and Training

The Administrator and Chairman of the Personnel Committee, with the assistance of early childhood education specialists, will continually evaluate staff programs, facilities, and all areas of the operation, as it relates to staff. The Personnel Committee has the responsibility for suggesting staff training.

13. Medicals
The Day Care Act requires that each employee have a yearly medical stating that he or she is free of communicable diseases.

Training
Training new employees is necessary for the spirit, survival, and performance of the company as a whole. It generally involves upgrading technical skills, personal development skills, and human relations skills. Learning how to operate a computer terminal, write a business report, or conduct a performance appraisal are examples of training. The three steps in the training process are:

1) Conduct a "training needs assessment."

2) Set goals and criteria for the training activities. This includes establishing short-term and long-term objectives, and the criteria for evaluating the programs.

3) Program evaluation provides an important assessment of the training process. Evaluation occurs during three stages: a) while training, b) at the end of the training program, and c) after a length of time back on the job.

After hiring, orientation and training are the key to establishing positive performance. Concentrate on this procedure to maximize your valuable new resource. Chapter Nine completes the hiring loop, testing your selection decision through performance appraisals.

CHAPTER NINE
Testing Your Decision — Performance Appraisals

Previous chapters discussed how employees are selected and trained. This last chapter will examine how hiring decisions can be tested through performance appraisals. A performance appraisal is an evaluation of the employee's performance on the job.

Performance appraisals serve other functions as well.

1) Performance feedback allows the employee and the company to take appropriate steps to improve performance.

2) Appraisals help decision-makers determine who should receive pay raises. Many companies base pay increases and bonuses solely on merit, which is guaged primarily through performance appraisals.

3) Promotions, transfers, and demotions are usually based on past or anticipated performance. Often promotions are a reward for past performance.

4) Poor performance may indicate the need for retraining. Likewise, good performance may indicate untapped potential that could be further developed.

5) Performance appraisals can guide career decisions, indicating which paths are most appropriate.

6) Poor performance may be symptomatic of an ill-conceived job design. Appraisals help uncover such errors.

Although these six uses of performance appraisals are important, the key point is that they can be utilized as the main tool for evaluating previous hiring decisions. The performance appraisal is designed to flesh out an accurate picture of an individual's job performance over a predetermined period of time.

To achieve this, appraisals must be job-related, practical, standardized, and measurable. Job-related means that the appraisal evaluates key behaviors that constitute job success, as defined by the job description. A job-related approach must also be practical. A practical system is one that is understood by all evaluators and employees. A complicated, impractical approach may result in resentment and nonuse. Confusion can also lead to inaccuracies that reduce the effectiveness of the appraisal as a tool.

The procedure should also be standardized. To illustrate a well thought out performance appraisal, I have enclosed one that was designed for employees enrolled in an apprenticeship program for a large utility company.

Performance Appraisal and Development Guide

The main purposes of the performance appraisal program are to provide an equitable method to:

1. help in fairly assessing an employee's job performance and communicate this information to the employee;
2. help in identifying the development needs of employees and appropriate actions which can be used to improve job performance;
3. serve as a guide to fairness and equity in salary administration.

The performance appraisal form is designed to assist in formulating and recording valid appraisals of the degree to which employees have achieved expected job results.

The performance appraisal and development guide form provides for:

1. identifying the job performance factors that are reflected in job results;
2. evaluating the achievement of results in the controllable job performance factors;
3. evaluating the employee's overall understanding of his or her job;
4. evaluating overall job performance;
5. identifying employee performance develpment needs;
6. identifying specific development actions to help improve each individual's job performance.

-1-

JOB PERFORMANCE FACTORS

The key job performance factors which are reflected in job results are:

QUANTITY	Amount, volume of acceptable work. Achievement of results.
QUALITY	Accuracy, thoroughness, completeness, preciseness. Usefulness of results. Degree to which results reflect new concepts, approaches or applications.
TIMELINESS	Assignments, projects, reports completed on or ahead of schedule or plan.
COST	Degree of effectiveness in using resources. Minimizing controllable costs in own work and its effect on others. Optimization of controllable costs, the establishment and/or meeting of cost standards or budgets.
SAFETY	Observance of safe working practices; avoidance of lost time accidents. Development and maintenance of safe working environment and facilities; prevention of lost time accidents; appropriate corrective actions.
DEVELOPMENT OF OTHERS	Selecting subordinates, evaluating their job performance, identifying improvement needs, and using work assignments for development purposes. Instructing, guiding or directing others, motivating them to improve their performance.

-2-

JOB PERFORMANCE RESULTS GUIDE

The degree of achievement, compared with expected results may be:

RESULTS WELL BELOW STANDARD	Performance results show consistent deficiencies which seriously interfere with the attainment of job objectives.
IMPROVED RESULTS NEEDED	Performance results show generally inconsistent achievement of job objectives; performance improvement is needed.
STANDARDS MET	Performance results show consistent achievement of objectives.
STANDARDS EXCEEDED	Performance results show consistent achievement of objectives.
OUTSTANDING	Performance results consistently above standard with overall performance substantially above objectives.

Note: Standards will vary for different kinds and levels of positions, and in each instance the supervisor should refer to the position description to determine a reasonable standard.

-3-

A — JOB PERFORMANCE APPRAISAL

Name of Employee: ____________________

Due Date: ____________________

Job Title: ____________________

Period of Appraisal Review: ____________________
(From) (To)

Supervisor's Name: ____________________

Time Under Your Supervision: ____________________

I. JOB PERFORMANCE RESULTS

Describe the RESULTS achieved compared with RESULTS expected. Focus on each job performance factor (QUANTITY, QUALITY, TIMELINESS, COST, SAFETY, DEVELOPMENT OF OTHERS) relative to major objectives, projects or assignments.

Consider the individual's understanding of his role in relation to that part of the overall corporate objectives assigned to your work area.

Make any additional comments which will clarify your overall evaluation, e.g.: circumstances that affected job performance beyond the employee's control, reassignment, etc. ____________________

B — INDIVIDUAL DEVELOPMENT GUIDE

Name of Employee: ______________________

Due Date: ______________________

Job Title: ______________________

Period of Appraisal Review: ______________________
(From) (To)

Supervisor's Name: ______________________

Time Under Your Supervision: ______________________

I. PERFORMANCE DEVELOPMENT NEEDS AND COUNSELLING

A. For each of the Job Performance Factors listed below, indicate any shortcomings or development needs the employee has in the managerial skills shown in the matrix. For example, consider the performance factor of QUANTITY. If the employee's performance results indicate a need for improvement in the QUANTITY factor and the reasons for the results are due to shortcomings in Planning and Know-how, check those two skills in the matrix. Next consider the job performance factor of QUALITY, etc.

Managerial Skills / Job Performance Factors	Planning	Organizing	Directing	Controlling	Communi-cations	Relationships With Others	Know-how	Staffing
Quantity								
Quality								
Timeliness								
Cost								
Safety								
Development of Others								

B. Describe the needs identified above as hindering the achievement of standard or above standard results. ______

C. Is the employee in the RIGHT JOB? Are there other areas in which his or her skills and capabilities could be more effectively utilized? Explain. ______

Employee Name: ______________________________

Department: ______________________________

Division: ______________ District: ______________

INDIVIDUAL DEVELOPMENT ACTION

II. PERFORMANCE DEVELOPMENT

Consider the employee's development need described in Section I and recommend specific development actions which you believe will help the employee to *improve his or her performance*. If you believe that on-the-job training is the only or best development action to help an employee improve performance, identify that as the development action.

Development Action	Implementation Time (Start)	(Completion)
______________________	__________	__________
______________________	__________	__________
______________________	__________	__________
______________________	__________	__________
______________________	__________	__________
______________________	__________	__________
______________________	__________	__________
______________________	__________	__________

III. GROWTH DEVELOPMENT

Consider the employee's development needs in terms of those development actions which will help him or her in *assuming greater responsibility* in the present position or in preparing for greater responsibility beyond the present job.

Development Action	Implementation Time (Start)	(Completion)

Prepared by: ______________________

Reviewed by: ______________________

Date Discussed with Employee: ______________

Employee Name:		
Department:	Division:	District:
Payroll Location	Employee Number	Social Security Number

I. JOB PERFORMANCE RESULTS (Continued from page 4)

II. EFFECT OF EMPLOYEE'S PERFORMANCE ON RESULTS OF OTHERS

- [ ] Results achieved had the normally acceptable effect on objectives and results of other employees or organizations.
- [ ] Results achieved contributed most favorably to the objectives and results of other employees and organizations.
- [ ] Results achieved were to the detriment of objectives and results of other employees or organizations.

-9-

Explain: ____________________

____

____

____

____

____

____

____

____

____

III. OVERALL JOB PERFORMANCE DURING THE APPRAISAL PERIOD

Overall Results Well Below Standard	Improved Results Needed	Overall Standards Met	Overall Standards Exceeded	Outstanding
☐ 1	☐ 2	☐ 3	☐ 4	☐ 5

Prepared by: ____________________

Reviewed by: ____________________

Date Counselling Scheduled: ____________________

Date Discussed with Employee: ____________________

A signed copy of this form is to be given to the employee at the time of his or her performance counselling.

The following ten guidelines will assist you in conducting performance appraisal interviews:

1) Formally review performance at least once a year — preferably twice a year.
2) Reassure each employee that the purpose of the performance appraisal session is to improve performance and foster better communication, not to discipline.
3) Conduct the performance review session in private with a minimum of interruptions.
4) Recognize positive aspects of the employee's performance.
5) Make criticisms specific. Don't be vague.
6) Focus criticism on performance, not personality characteristics.
7) Refuse to argue with the perfon you are evaluating.
8) Emphasize the evaluator's willingness to assist the employee's effort, and to improve performance.
9) Identify specific actions the employee can take to improve performance.
10) Terminate the session by reiterating the positive aspects of the employee's performance.

Perhaps the most significant challenge raised by the performance appraisal is for the company to integrate the feedback from these appraisals into the staff selection process. Managers need to be keenly aware of poor performance, especially when it is widespread or the result of past hiring decisions, whose consequences are still being felt.

Conclusion

Now that you have read this book, keep referring to it as a constant source of practical information, to ensure that you never have to pay the price of a poor hiring decision. Once you have the basic knowledge of hiring, the odds of being successful are in your favour. I sincerely hope that this manual will help you be successful in your future hiring endeavours.

ORDER FORM

❑ **Yes,** please send me _____ copy/copies of ***How to Hire the Right Person the First Time,*** $19.95 each

(please print)
Name: ______________________

Organization: ______________________

Address: ______________________

City: __________ Province/State: __________

Postal Code/Zip Code: ______________________

Telephone: __________ Fax: __________

❑ Send more information on Denis' services

❑ We require a speaker for (list date & topic): __________

M
Vi
Ch
In
1X
66

Denis L. Cauvier Seminars
26 Boyd Avenue
Enfield, Nova Scotia
Canada B0N 1N0
(902) 883-7636

Newport Marketing & Communications Inc.

Titles of related publications from Newport Marketing & Communications Inc.:

Complete Programs — Casettes, tapes and books:	Price
1. *Marketing Your Business from the Inside-Out* (six tapes)	$94.95
2. *Building Sales Excellence from the Inside-Out* (six tapes)	$94.95
3. *Increase Your Restaurant Sales from the Inside-Out* (six tapes)	$94.95
4. *Uncover and Create Additional Business Opportunities* (four tapes)	$74.95

Speaking of Business — Single Tapes:	
1. Discover Business Opportunities	$14.95
2. Personal Excellence Spells Success	$14.95
3. Sales Excellence from the Inside-Out	$14.95
4. Phone Power	$14.95
5. Management Excellence	$14.95
6. Super Service Spells Success	$14.95
7. Marketing from the Inside-Out	$14.95
8. Monitor Yourself and Worry Management	$14.95
9. Drop the Role and Go for the Goal	$14.95
10. Power of Attitude and Contact Opportunities	$14.95
11. Telephone Handling and Closing the Sale	$14.95